Multifaith Chaplaincy
in the Workplace

of related interest

Talking about Spirituality in Health Care Practice
A Resource for the Multi-Professional Health Care Team
Gillian White
ISBN 978 1 84310 305 9
eISBN 978 1 84642 493 9

Spiritual Care in Practice
Case Studies in Healthcare Chaplaincy
Edited by George Fitchett and Steve Nolan
ISBN 978 1 84905 976 3
eISBN 978 0 85700 876 3

Multifaith Care for Sick and Dying Children and their Families
A Multi-disciplinary Guide
Paul Nash, Madeleine Parkes and Zamir Hussain
ISBN 978 1 84905 606 9
eISBN 978 1 78450 072 6

MULTIFAITH
CHAPLAINCY
in the
WORKPLACE

*How Chaplains Can Support
Organizations and their
Employees*

Fiona Stewart-Darling

Jessica Kingsley *Publishers*
London and Philadelphia

Quotes on the following pages reproduced with
kind permission of the following:
Pages 33–4 Matt Hammerstein, Barclays
Page 37 Sir David Walker
Alan Smith
Page 69 Moshe Freedman
Pages 69, 70–1 Shaykh Ibrahim Mogra
The Tanenbaum Centre

First published in 2017
by Jessica Kingsley Publishers
73 Collier Street
London N1 9BE, UK
and
400 Market Street, Suite 400
Philadelphia, PA 19106, USA

www.jkp.com

Library of Congress Cataloging in Publication Data
Title: Multifaith chaplaincy in the workplace / Fiona Stewart-Darling.
Description: Philadelphia : Jessica Kingsley Publishers, 2017. | Includes
bibliographical references.
Identifiers: LCCN 2016055064 (print) | LCCN 2017008456 (ebook) | ISBN
9781785920295 (alk. paper) | ISBN 9781784502799 (ebook)
Subjects: LCSH: Religion in the workplace. | Chaplains.
Classification: LCC BL65.W67 S74 2017 (print)
| LCC BL65.W67 (ebook) | DDC
206/.1--dc23

British Library Cataloguing in Publication Data
A CIP catalogue record for this book is available from the British Library

ISBN 978 1 78592 029 5
eISBN 978 1 78450 279 9

Printed and bound in Great Britain

In memory of
Alan Stewart-Darling
(1931–2015)

Contents

Acknowledgements

I am grateful to Bishop Adrian Newman and the Canary Wharf Chaplaincy Steering Group for granting me study leave in the autumn of 2014 when this book began to take shape, through the writing of two articles. I am grateful to the director, staff and community of scholars with whom I shared my study leave at The Collegeville Institute, Minnesota, USA, for their constructive suggestions, particularly at the seminar I led on my work. I'm grateful also for the grants and people who contributed to making my study leave possible.

Thanks must also go to Sir George Iacobescu CEO and Chairman of the Canary Wharf Group, Bishop Richard Chartres and Bishop Stephen Oliver, who took the risk of inviting me to create the Canary Wharf Multifaith Chaplaincy. There are many people I have journeyed with both in the wharf and outside since I began this task, who have educated me, challenged my thinking and generously spent time with me and to whom I owe a huge thank you. I am also grateful for the companies who have generously embraced and supported the work of the chaplaincy.

There are so many people who have encouraged me and supported the chaplaincy, too numerous to mention by name. However, there a few without whom this work would not have been possible: Lord Stephen Green, Sir David Walker, the members of the Chaplaincy Steering Group both past and present, my chaplaincy colleagues, who have had to put up with me not always being around as I have spent time completing the manuscript, Jane Tappenden, Vladimir Felzmann, Moshe Freedman, Ibrahim Mogra, Geoff Nicholson and our newest team member, Natalie Debloux.

And thanks of course to family and friends, who have had to put up with me being busier than normal over the last couple of years and, I suspect, will look forward to me having more time to play! I am grateful for the continued support and encouragement my parents have given me in all the jobs and projects I have undertaken. Sadly, my father died several weeks after I returned from study leave, but at least I had the chance to explain the outlines of the articles I had written during that time. And finally, I thank Jenny, whose gentle encouragement has helped me to complete this book. I have been very fortunate to have such a good and supportive editor in Natalie Watson.

Introduction

As I set out to write this book, it is important to state why I'm doing it, particularly when there are so many books about chaplaincy already written; why another one? Many of the books written to date are either a brief survey of different types of chaplaincy, or they tend to be mainly about healthcare chaplaincy. In writing about my particular chaplaincy expertise in the workplace I believe that I have something new and unique to say.

In writing this book I will argue that far from disappearing from our society, faith and religion are still very much present and an important part of many people's lives, as well as active in the public arena. This has been my experience, having spent a number of years working as a chaplain within the financial and professional services industry. During this time, I have become aware of an increasing open generosity towards religion and belief and the distinctive role chaplaincy can play in the workplace. It is my hope that business leaders as well as leaders of faith communities will read this book, and that it might also prove useful for anyone, whether they have a faith or not.

Chaplaincy, in particular multifaith chaplaincy, is well established within hospitals, prisons and universities, all of which have their own models. Following the decline of the manufacturing industry in the UK (known as Industrial Mission), had all but disappeared. However, in recent years, this trend has been reversed and more and more chaplains can be found in different workplace contexts. Chaplaincy is now found within retail malls, city centres, airports and other places of work. However, the majority of workplace chaplaincy initiatives have come from the Christian churches and are being undertaken mostly by volunteers.

For me, it is important to tell the Canary Wharf Multifaith Chaplaincy story, because it is unique in being multifaith from the outset, working with global companies in East London and operating within the bounds of a private business park. Through it being multifaith, my colleagues and I have discovered that it has enabled us to speak openly and with integrity about faith and how it can positively impact the workplace and contribute to the wellbeing of employees and their behaviour.

Within this book I describe how I developed the model for multifaith chaplaincy within Canary Wharf; how it relates to and supports global businesses; why the businesses need chaplaincy; and why a multifaith chaplaincy is able to make a greater impact and contribution than a solely Christian one.

In establishing the chaplaincy it was important to understand from the beginning the context and challenges companies and employees face. So in Chapter 1, I describe some of the issues we encountered, such as living within a fast and changing world, where technology is evolving constantly, continuing to change the way business operates. Economic activity is global and other new economies are beginning to emerge and contribute to the global economy. This has implications for the workforce, which is becoming more diverse in terms of nationality, cultures and faith. It would be hard to write a book telling the story of setting up a chaplaincy for the business community – in my particular context for the financial and professional service industries – without mention of the contributing factors of the global financial crisis. Surprisingly, this created a number of positive opportunities for the fledgling chaplaincy.

Chapter 2 tells the story of the evolving chaplaincy, its challenges and opportunities. It explores how faith is becoming more prominent in the public arena and in the life of companies, particularly around enshrining religion within UK employment law and as a strand of the diversity and inclusion agenda of many organizations. The establishing of the chaplaincy was a long-term project dependant on building strong relationships with the companies through getting to know individuals. At the same time, it was a process of patiently helping companies to understand that they could no longer just have a nodding acquaintance with faith in the workplace in terms of ensuring that people of faith were not discriminated against, and that faith can could no longer be ignored or side-lined and could have a positive influence on the working environment.

As I mentioned earlier, the majority of workplace chaplaincy initiatives have come from the Christian churches, within both the UK and the USA. However, in my experience the reason the chaplaincy in Canary Wharf has become firmly embedded is that it is truly multifaith. In Chapter 3, I explore why building a multifaith team is important, given that we live in a globalized world where 80 per cent of the population adhere to a religion and there is much movement of the workforce between countries and indeed continents which has an impact on employees' expectations within the workplace.

Another important factor is that as companies seek to set up office bases outside Europe, often they find themselves in a country that is overtly religious and they have to learn to navigate the challenges that this presents. I explore also the added value that multifaith chaplaincy can bring to the workplace, with reflections from both my Muslim and Jewish colleagues. Finally, I comment on the role of the established Church of England, the opportunities it presents in facilitating and supporting people of all faiths and its contribution in helping to shape the work and ethos of chaplaincy.

As a multifaith chaplaincy team we are committed to offer assistance in promoting the role and value of wisdom from a faith perspective, as it helps to bring a more integrated approach and give a wider context to values and ethics. One of the consequences of the global financial crisis was that global banks had to change and improve their internal cultures and ensure that the right values and ethics were embedded throughout their organizations. This was driven by the regulators and the need to restore public trust. It provided an ideal opportunity to engage with the companies and have conversations around drawing on wisdom, which has a long tradition within many world faiths. In Chapter 4, I recount some of the challenges, issues and ideas around the role of wisdom alongside ethics, values and culture and how we can help people make the best decision possible when the issue is not black and white (as is the case with the majority of business decisions).

There is much anxiety around allowing religion within the workplace, and in Chapter 5 I explore the main concerns. The biggest concern is around the issues of proselytizing, as both Christianity and Islam are concerned with making converts. I explore a wider definition of mission within faith and how fruitful conversations within and between religions can be possible, within a framework of hospitality and embassy. Often there is much misunderstanding about religion, or even between religions, and so mature and adult discussions are important in learning to respect and value each other, as well as living comfortably with differences of opinions.

In Chapter 6, I explore why faith communities need to support chaplains and why chaplains need the support and encouragement of their faith communities. How can chaplains act as translators of the world to their particular faith communities and how can their faith communities inform their theology and work as a chaplain?

And finally in the Conclusion, I follow the principle of open questions, offering some themes and topics either for individual or group exploration from the perspective of different faiths. I suggest themes that are related to work and the economy and how we might equip people of faith within the workplace to have a more informed understanding.

I have tried to write a helpful account of the establishing and work of the Canary Wharf Multifaith Chaplaincy and the increasing role that faith plays within public life, which I hope will be read by both business and faith leaders. I am aware that as a Christian chaplain and as a Church of England priest, much of what I have reflected on and shared has been through the Christian lens, but I hope that I have given enough material to enable food for thought for the intended wider audience.

1

Welcome to My World

In developing any kind of ministry or business it is important to understand the local and wider context and environment in which it will operate. This is particularly true for chaplains, who essentially work on someone else's territory. In order to develop a chaplaincy that is able to function and deliver relevant activities, we need to understand the world in which the chaplaincy will operate, the challenges and issues that people and businesses face. Chaplains will also need to be aware of the boundaries in which they can operate, and adhere to them, as well as respecting the culture and working environments. It is therefore important that chaplains listen and try to understand the world they inhabit and in which they seek to offer engagement from a faith perspective. In this chapter, I want to give a brief overview of the rapidly changing world we inhabit and, in particular, the unique context of Canary Wharf, the nature of the companies and workforce and the complexity of the challenges and issues they face.

Canary Wharf is located in the East End of London. It has been described on the internet in the following way:

> Canary Wharf is the [new] financial centre located in the East End of London. It is worth visiting this outstanding example of regeneration which provides a first class working, shopping and leisure environment.

It is a showcase of many modern architectural styles set in the old docklands environment.[1]

Canary Wharf is a global financial centre and an extension of the City of London. Every day billions of pounds in equities and currency are traded through offices in Canary Wharf – and investment decisions are made which support businesses across the globe. In developing a workplace multifaith chaplaincy which is appropriate for this setting it has been essential to understand what this means for the people who work here, given its local and global nature.

The world of Canary Wharf

Recently I attended a team meeting of a group within a human resource department of one of the global American banks. The team meeting was for about 16 people. Eight of the team were in the room; the remainder were linked via video conferencing from places such as Russia, Turkey, the United Arab Emirates, South Africa, Poland and Bulgaria. The managing director who had invited me to the meeting had a remit for the EMEA (Europe, Middle East and Africa) side of the business, which covers roughly 50 countries.[2]

To assist with understanding the wider context of the Canary Wharf Multifaith Chaplaincy, here is a flavour of the mixture of the companies based within the Canary Wharf estate. They are mainly from the financial and professional services, although that is starting to change as financial technology companies are increasingly attracted to set up offices in Canary Wharf. The companies based on the estate range from global bank headquarters such as Barclays and HSBC, EMEA (Europe Middle East and Africa) bank headquarters for American banks such as Citi, Morgan Stanley, JP Morgan, international law firms, professional service companies such as KPMG and Ernst Young, rating agencies S&P, Moody's and Fitch, and oil companies Shell and BP. Companies continue to relocate to Canary Wharf and future tenants will include Deutsche Bank and Société Générale. All these businesses operate locally and nationally as well as across national boundaries, like so many other business sectors.

London is a multicultural city where over 300 different languages are spoken. The international working population of the private business park known as Canary Wharf reflects this diverse multicultural and multifaith community, as does the way business is now conducted. Companies operate in many countries and a number of their functions can be easily outsourced from London to less expensive locations; for example, one of the American banks has outsourced a large part of its human resources department to Belfast. This has been made possible in part by the continued technological developments, as I experienced in my recent meeting described earlier, when it was almost as if we were all sitting in the same room. Business can be conducted almost anywhere, especially now with the huge sophisticated advances in information technology (IT), including smartphones and tablets with their capabilities and internet access, making communications rapid if not instantaneous around the world.

Canary Wharf is important for the UK and world economies. Like the City of London and other centres around the UK, it contributes to making the UK the leading exporter of financial and professional services across the world. Foreign companies have invested over £100 billion in the UK financial services sector since 2007, close to a third of total foreign direct investment (FDI). Financial services attract more FDI into the UK than any other sector (The City UK 2016).

Another significant factor is that the working population in Canary Wharf has grown from 60,000 from when I began the chaplaincy in 2004 to its current figure of approximately 115,000, and will continue to grow to about 200,000 when the estate is finished in the next ten years or so. However, it is important to note that not all those employed on the estate work in the glass towers. There is a significant retail business, with over 300 shops, cafes and restaurants, making it the fourth largest shopping destination within the M25. In addition, there is a significant security team as well as many construction workers continuing to develop the estate.

In Canary Wharf, security is a daily issue; a high security presence is visible externally on the estate and within all the buildings. It is impossible to enter any of the buildings without a prior appointment. While the majority of this book will focus on chaplaincy to the businesses, it has been important for us to also understand the challenges that retail workers face in terms of the chaplaincy services we offer them. In particular, in 2013, when unidentified gunmen attacked the Westgate shopping mall in Nairobi, Kenya, the retail workers in Canary Wharf became very nervous given that most of the malls are below street level. They needed to be reassured. This was the responsibility of the estate owners Canary Wharf Group, but the chaplaincy played an important part in offering such reassurance. In many ways Canary Wharf is a microcosm of the wider business scene.

Living in a global world

Globalization has meant that the world we live in has expanded and shrunk at the same time. Every aspect of our lives is influenced by the fact we live in the global world. More and more companies operate in multiple locations in different countries, and international commuting by executives is an everyday occurrence. We are dependant on a global economy for our daily needs. For example, according to the Food Standards Agency[3] 50 per cent of food consumed in the UK is imported from countries outside the UK. Many of the clothes we wear will be made in another country, or designed by a UK company but made in other parts of the world where the cost of labour is significantly cheaper than in the UK.

However, this does not mean that the fear expressed by some of being controlled from outside our own country has become any less. In the summer of 2016 a referendum was held about the UK's relationship to the European Union (EU), the vote to leave or to remain. It was surprising that a number of political leaders from around the world felt it was important to offer their opinion as to how Britain should vote, a statement more about Britain's standing in the world markets than a desire to manipulate its politicians. These comments were by and large not appreciated by the British public, many of whom argued that they didn't like to be told what to do and wanted their sovereignty back. At the same time, there was a rise in violent crime against immigrants and a growing anxiety about what the consequences of Britain leaving the EU would be. We live in a global world, and although some political decisions appear to be local or national, actually there are implications that reach beyond a nation's borders.

We also live in a world that appears less secure than before. Security is a huge concern in today's world. In the UK, as I write this, the current threat of international terrorism is considered 'severe', which means an attack is highly likely, and the current threat level from Northern Ireland-related terrorism in Britain is 'substantial', which means an attack is a strong possibility. Every day we just have to turn on the news to find that there has been a terrorist attack somewhere in the world. The attack on the twin towers in New York on 9/11 changed the world, and the UK was changed with the 7/7 attacks in London in 2005. News about foiled or actual terror attacks in parts of the Western world, on our doorstep, seems to have become a much more frequent occurrence.

The world too has become smaller. In the last 30 years, information technology and social media have totally changed the way in which people communicate and receive information. If we think in terms of world news, it is instant. Something happens on the other side of the world, and it is very quickly known in this part of the world, not just through dedicated news channels but through social media, including people sending their own personal viral videos and live streaming. We have a world where information is made available really quickly; people's immediate reactions and thoughts are broadcast through Twitter or other forms of social media the minute they are conceived. In the last ten years also, there has been an explosion of different types of social media made possible through the introduction of smartphones and tablets, enabling people to access the internet on the move or wherever they happen to be.

According to the Pew Research Center (2016), 62 per cent of all Americans access the news using social media sites such as Facebook, Twitter, Reddit and Tumblr. YouTube also has an important role to play in obtaining news. The Pew Research Center has conducted research about how different generations obtain the news, particularly political news. Millennials (those born in the 1990s) have relatively low reliance on local TV, which almost mirrors the Baby Boomers' (those born from 1946 to the mid-1960s) comparatively low reliance on Facebook. Generation Xs (born from the mid-1960s to the early 1980s) bridge the gap between the Millennials and the Baby Boomers, roughly half Generation Xs get political news on Facebook and about half use local TV (Mitchell 2015).

Facebook continues to be the most used social media and reached one billion users in 2012.[4] It is also very interesting how quickly things get tweeted, and what kind of things are tweeted, even with a limit of 140 characters. WhatsApp is another very popular social media application, alongside Instagram, Snapchat and Pinterest, to name but a few.

As I illustrated earlier in this chapter, information technology has also enabled instant communication within global companies with the employees based in different countries around the world. This has contributed to the changes in my context and setting as a chaplain in a leading financial hub in the financial sector. In particular, 27 October 1986 saw deregulation of the London Stock Market. On that date, a number of changes occurred, including a shift from a physical human-based activity to reliance on a system using electronic exchange. This enabled faster trading and more immediate results and changed the way people approached economic work and the pattern of their days. The growth in information technology continues to influence the way industries and businesses review and develop their working practices.

Another phenomenon that has increased since the turn of the century is the number of people who are part of online or virtual communities through social media. This has for some become the means for searching for housemates or flatmates, or for finding their soulmate who might then become their spouse. While there are many good and helpful things about social media, there is also a downside in that it can provide an easy if not secretive way to fuel negative behaviour such as addiction or gambling or pornography. People lead often very stressful lives with long hours at work and long commutes, all of which can put pressure on relationships. While smartphones and tablets enable people to keep in close contact, often we encounter people walking down the street or on the train apparently talking to themselves, when in fact they are in the middle of a telephone conversation. These devices enable people to keep in contact with their online communities.

In my early days as chaplain in Canary Wharf I discovered that, although based in London, managers were making decisions that had global consequences. I was told of the pressures that arise from working globally, with virtually 24-hour trading on the financial markets. One executive told me that he was at his desk at 7am as he worked with Australian markets and another told me that he was at his desk until the New York Stock Exchange closed at 9pm. There are only two hours in any 24-hour period when there is no electronic trading anywhere in the world.

Global economies are connected. A slowdown in the growth rate of China's economy has a global effect. The credit crunch, or the global financial crisis, had global consequences. Our world is interconnected.

Workforces in global companies are made up of people from many different cultural and religious backgrounds. In the workplace, people work in teams with those whom they might not normally come across in other areas of their lives. There are different genders, nationalities, ethnicity, religions and ages. The workplace has always been a place where different generations have worked side by side. It is changing as people are expected to work longer, with a later retirement age; this is not only true for the business sector but is the case across many professions and jobs. We will continue to experience the age gap between those starting their working lives and those finishing, as the retirement age continues to increase with increased life expectancy. The Harvard Business Review in 2013 said that for the first time in history, five generations will soon be working side by side (Knight 2014).

Currently we tend to classify the workforce as Baby Boomers, Generation Xs and the Generation Ys or the Millennials. These three generations view the world very differently, have different learning styles and contrasting motivations, attitudes and ambitions. While the observations of these different generations should not be taken as being held hard and fast, generally Baby Boomers and Generation Xs may favour more traditional and static training methods like *PowerPoint* presentations and handbooks, while younger workers may gravitate towards a more interactive and technology-based form of learning and sharing information. The younger generations tend to be much more tech savvy as they have grown up with it and it is a normal part of their lives, whereas the Baby Boomers have embraced technology but not to the same extent.

The world is changing and the notion of a job for life in one place is no longer the norm; many who are entering the workforce today will have a number of careers before they retire. This in turn means that the Millennials are less loyal to their company and are less inclined to work a 60-hour week, which Baby Boomers feel is a prerequisite for success. Many hard-working Millennials want more of a work–life balance, and will occasionally work overtime but also want their weekends to be work free. They are highly skilled at making technology work for them, for example they may voluntarily choose to make up the time in unstructured settings like working in a cafe. As a Baby Boomer myself, I have been interested to see how the Millennials are changing the workplace and challenging the well-established status quo of my generation and that of Generation X. While Baby Boomers will often put up with something as a means to an end, Millennials want to find a sense of meaning and purpose in what they are doing. They do not see it as a job for life, but more of a 'tour of duty' and the reality is that not only will they have number of jobs but also different careers before they retire. This has challenging implications for those professions which are still expecting those they train to stay for the whole of their working lives. The increased level of mobility and expectations will inevitably have an impact on personal attitudes, behaviours and beliefs and how they contribute to both the workplace and wider society.

It is interesting to mention here something that I will later expand on. Despite the evidence that in the West, faith in terms of personal adherence seems to be on a downward trend, faith in the public arena seems to be on the upward trend, and I will discuss reasons for this later. But it is worth mentioning a few pointers here. While the culture in the UK is changing, essentially the working week is still Monday to Friday with the opportunity for leisure activities at weekends. Although this is changing, particularly with regard to Sunday trading,

Christians in the UK and the USA are free to worship on Sundays. Also, given the nature of multiculturalism and global movement of workforces, in many places it is recognized that special arrangements need to be made for Muslims in the workplace on Fridays, and similar arrangements for Jews, particularly for the winter months. Faith cannot be ignored in the global business arena. With global companies having offices all over the world they need to be aware of local cultures. For example, if they have offices in Muslim countries, their offices will be closed on Fridays, and Sunday is a normal working day. Companies need to take care that they operate within local religious laws. In addition, in Muslim countries they will operate according to the Muslim calendar of festivals. However, in North America, Europe and other countries that have Christian origins, these countries operate according to the Christian calendar festivals. Because of globalization, faith and religion cannot be ignored in the workplace, even in a secular post-Christian country like the UK.

How and where do people belong?

A pregnant young woman asked to see me for a coffee. During our conversation she mentioned the potential conflict she and her husband were experiencing as they both had different ideas about where they would bring up their child. She was Australian and wanted to go back home, and he was from Norway and wanted to bring his child up there. This is just one of the many issues working within an international business community and living within a multicultural city brings up. Where do people call home? Potentially this couple could call three different countries home.

When I was in my early twenties and thirties, I was often asked where my home was. My answer was always that it was where I happened to be living at the time, that was my home. However, in most instances, the question being asked was really where I grew up and where my parents lived. I think today, particularly in a global city like London, asking someone where their home is, is more about asking them where they feel they belong, where they have put down roots. Many people today, particularly the young, live much more transient lives and are much more flexible in terms of where they live, how often they change their job or change the company they work for, and sometimes the country in which they live.

Many people working in Canary Wharf commute reasonable distances across Greater London. It is not unusual to have a daily commute of up to an hour-and-a-half each way, or even more, with some people commuting weekly from other parts of the UK or further afield.

Most people belong to a number of communities, some of which overlap and some of which do not, and this is increased given that most people commute to work. These communities may include the workplace, where people live, the sports club, the gym, the local wine bar or pub. Interestingly, people of faith, and in particular Christians, will often belong to a number of faith communities, for example their local church, a church near their workplace and the workplace Christian fellowship. For this reason, I often talk about support and ministry at both ends of the commuter line. For those of us who belong to a faith community, it is often to them that we turn for help. So if someone is commuting daily from Grantham in Lincolnshire, and their husband is in hospital, then it is easier for a member of their local church to pick the children up from school than for a work colleague in London to do this.

A survey by the *Independent* newspaper claimed that:

> Almost a quarter of those questioned have lived in 10 or more homes in their lives with moving unsurprisingly more common among younger people – 54 per cent of people aged under 25 have already lived in three or more places. On average, people typically move three more times before they are 45.
>
> (*Independent* 2013)

These days, people move around a lot. In the part of London where I live it is estimated that many of the professionals move after three years, and couples with children nearing secondary school age move out of London. This has a knock-on effect for the stability of local communities and an impact on an individual's ability to belong.

The role of the global financial crisis – an unexpected consequence

> The clergy of the City of London have been in the front line of pastoral care. The same is true of Fiona Stewart-Darling and her responsibility as the Bishop's Chaplain on Canary Wharf where the day-time parish numbers about 100,000 people. It is difficult to know whether to sympathize more with those who have lost their jobs or those who are left carrying even greater loads with higher targets and fewer colleagues.
>
> (General Synod 2009)

I developed the chaplaincy for this specialized business community by building relationships. These relationships helped me to gain insights into the challenges, issues and pressures facing companies and individuals working across a range of businesses in Canary Wharf. I discovered that although based in London, managers were making decisions of such magnitude that they had global consequences. I was told of the pressures that arise from working globally. Early on in establishing the chaplaincy I had a conversation with a banker who commuted every other week to New York, and he complained that it ate into his weekend because he travelled on Sunday. I asked why he travelled on Sunday rather than Monday morning and he replied that he thought it was expected of him. I then asked if he had had this conversation with his line manager, and he said no. I mentioned this to a senior executive in another company who said that they did not expect their employees to travel routinely on Sundays. Through this and other conversations I discovered that many people felt pressures and assumptions about their job and expectations to work long hours and did not question it. Most would say that they struggled to maintain a quality of life outside work; others struggled with balancing work and caring for young children or elderly sick parents. What became very clear was that people found it hard to leave these issues outside the workplace.

About three years into this project, I began to have conversations with managers who told me they had sleepless nights as they agonized over who in their team deserved a bonus and how much to award. Their companies had changed the parameters for bonus allocations and the pot was smaller. In other conversations I heard how companies were tightening their belts with the result that managers were planning and implementing restructures and organizational changes resulting in job losses. It soon became evident that we were on the brink of a global financial crisis. Fortunately, now I was in the privileged position of having relationships in place that enabled me to view the crisis from within the financial sector, which gave me a different perspective from the one portrayed by the media. I remember talking with a senior executive the day after a bank was declared bankrupt in September 2008. He told me how he and his colleagues had not been home for several days, but had stayed in the office trying to save the company and the employees' jobs. This sacrificial attitude portrayed a very different perspective from the media view of greedy bankers, and also amplified the emotional and moral responsibilities required of senior executives.

While it was obvious, as issues continued to emerge, that this was serious, through further conversations I became aware that the global financial crisis was a more complex disaster beyond the failures of the bankers and financial institutions. Nonetheless, the recklessness of some bank traders and systematic issues within the financial industry contributed to what has been described as the worst financial crisis for decades. I remember at this time being struck by the number of Christians, indeed people of all faiths, working within the financial services, and I heard the stories of criticism some had received from their faith communities for working in a bank. At the height of the crisis people were telling me that when they were asked where they worked, they did not want to say in a bank even if they were in a support role such as human resources or information technology. In my own conversations I found that the general public was unaware that many bank employees were not bankers, and there was a lack of understanding of the role of banks. It will take a long time for public trust to be restored in the banking industry.

One of the unexpected consequences of this time was that my relationships within the banks and other companies based in Canary Wharf were strengthened, as I was prepared to just be alongside managers and employees, willing to listen and be there for them. Human resource managers became more willing to advertise the chaplaincy services for their employees. This in turn led to individuals at all levels within companies seeking me out to chat informally over a coffee or a glass of wine. They discussed their struggles, either work related or personal. For them it was helpful to chat with someone outside their normal everyday sphere who would listen, was impartial and non-judgemental. Such conversations included speaking with a man who had begun to read substantial theological books and who wanted to discuss them with me, and supporting the deputy chief executive officer of a Swiss company and her colleagues through the closure of their London office. Other conversations focused on helping people to cope with abuse in marriage or bullying in the workplace. I have listened as senior executives or managers told me that they needed someone to talk to, because it is indeed lonely at the top, and I've chatted to security staff who have had to work when others have time off – they often work over Christmas and New Year and are away from their families.

As I write this I am aware that the financial and professional services are going through another period of uncertainty given a number of global economic factors – the slowing Chinese economy and lower oil prices to name just two important influences. I am also aware of the nervousness of the global, national and local business communities around the UK's decision to leave the EU, following the referendum.

What does your world look like?

I hope this chapter has given a helpful overview of the unique context of Canary Wharf and why exploring and understanding the context has been a fundamental starting point in developing the chaplaincy. I have explored how an awareness of the nature of the companies and workforce and the complexity of the challenges and issues they face daily has informed the development of a multifaith chaplaincy that is appropriate and at the same time maintains its integrity and critical awareness.

Before reading the next chapter, where I continue to cover in more detail the establishing of the chaplaincy, it might be helpful for the reader to pause and reflect on their own context. Whether you are a business leader making sense of the world in which you operate or a fellow chaplain thinking about either starting a new chaplaincy or developing an existing one and taking it to the next level, what does your world look like?

2

Why We Still Need Workplace Chaplaincy

Workplace chaplaincy is not new. It has its roots in what used to be called 'industrial mission', which really came into being after the Second World War with the armed forces chaplains returning to life within the Church. They became involved in chaplaincies to factories and other industries. Over the years, as our economic base has shifted away from manufacturing to more financial and service industries, chaplains have had to learn to adapt and find new ways of engaging with the workforce, understanding their context and the ever-changing world of business as it continues to be influenced by globalization, modern technology and changes in people's lifestyles and outlook on the world.

Religion in the public arena – space for a chaplaincy

For those that know it is there, the Chaplaincy is like the spirit of the Wharf – you may not be able to see it, but the knowledge that it is there to provide support in need is greatly reassuring; as it becomes truly multicultural (in principle and in practice), and awareness extends more widely, it has a real opportunity to become the soul of the Wharf – something many would suggest has been missing since its inception.

(Matt Hammerstein, Barclays)

The majority of people living in the West would agree that the place of religion in Western societies has changed significantly in the last few centuries. Secularization is a key element of modernity. The Canadian philosopher Charles Taylor (2007) examined this development and noticed that it is not a single, continuous transformation, but a series of new departures. He observes that the earlier forms of religious life have not totally been replaced by an absence of religion in today's secular world, although he would agree that in some societies religious belief and practice have markedly declined. Instead, there has been the continuing multiplication of new possibilities – religious, spiritual and anti-religious – giving individuals and groups space to make sense of their lives and shape to their spiritual aspirations. There has been a huge increase in spirituality and spiritual awareness; one just needs to go into most bookshops and see rows of self-help books encouraging people to discover themselves. Another aspect of modern society is that increasingly religious diversity is a reality, and distinctive in terms of the religious minorities now present in Britain. However, Grace Davie argues that 'British society is gradually sifting away from Christianity, but remains deeply coloured by it' (Davie 2015, p.223). The working community in Canary Wharf is international and very diverse and reflects attitudes to religion that can be very different from those in northern European and North American secular societies. Incidentally, I was amazed when I began the chaplaincy to see just how many Christians and people of other faiths worked in the financial sector, given the perception of the decline of personal faith as well as different perceptions as to what is by some considered an 'okay' profession for people of faith and not by others.

Religion is visible in the public arena in the UK, and is reflected in changes made to employment legislation. In December 2003, the Employment Equality (Religion or Belief) Regulations came into force. These outlawed direct and indirect discrimination and mean that employers are prevented from treating their staff less favourably than other staff on grounds of religious belief. In 2006, this was extended to cover the provision of goods and services. In 2007, the Equality and Human Rights Commission was established with responsibility by law for seven equality strands: age, disability, gender, race, religion or belief, sexual orientation and transgender. It then became a national human rights institution in 2009.

In 2004, when I was first beginning the chaplaincy and looking for ways to connect with the global companies, the inclusion of religion and belief into employment legislation was a gift, as companies were still trying to work out what it meant for them. While personal adherence to a faith seems to be on the decline, conversely faith and religion are now regularly being discussed on the public agenda, as evidenced by the recent Report of the Commission on Religion and Belief in British Public Life Living with Difference, chaired by The Rt Hon Baroness Elizabeth Butler-Sloss GBE (The Woolf Institute 2015).

This is also true in the business world. Indeed, the World Economic Forum, in one of its reports, made the following comment about religion and economic life:

> Faith permeates our world, providing a moral and ethical compass for the vast majority of people. Eight in ten people worldwide still identify with a religion. Evidence shows that – beyond individual religious practice – faith is increasingly moving into the public sphere and may affect various aspects of economic and social life. More and more often, people of faith are becoming key partners

in organizations aimed at tackling a varied set of global challenges – a sign of the important role of faith leaders and communities in bringing about social change.

(World Economic Forum 2014)

It makes a positive argument for the role of faith against the backdrop of an often distorted understanding of faith and religion which is the cause of much destruction, distress and pain within our world. Indeed, people with a religious faith, as the World Economic Forum has recognized, do not leave their faith at home – rather it is an important part of their daily lives and indeed can be a positive influence for good.

In the chaplaincy's early days many of the global companies made it clear that there was no room for religion in the workplace except for people of faith meeting informally in their faith groups. They complied with the employment legislation in secular countries such as the UK by ensuring that they had prayer rooms – at least the big companies did. Interestingly, there was and is no legal obligation within the legislation for companies to have prayer rooms. However, given the unique context of Canary Wharf and the evidence that religion and faith are very much part of the public arena, over time the companies' view of the role of chaplaincy began to slowly change as I patiently built relationships with the companies. Other factors that began to change the global banks' stance towards the chaplaincy had to do with external influences, in particular the pressure from governments' financial regulators to improve the culture within the financial industry as a direct result of the credit crunch in 2008. As the companies began to revise their stated values and ethics policies, and looked for ways to raise their employees' awareness of those policies, I began to explore with some business leaders the role that faith might play in these efforts. Much of our discussion had to do with the idea of wisdom, as it can shape the life of any community. Wisdom is a valued virtue in religious traditions and the secular world.

As a point of clarity, nowhere in this book is it intended to provide a critique of the banking culture of which much has been published, nor is the intention to offer an in-depth theological treatise. I mention the credit crunch because it offered a window for the chaplaincy to understand more of the continued process of changing the culture within institutions and individuals in the financial industry to help inform how the chaplains might engage and provide an appropriate model of chaplaincy. I believe chaplaincy provides a value added element for the companies and is not irrelevant to the economic aims of the companies in Canary Wharf.

How it all began

> For most of us working at Canary Wharf, a greater part of our day is necessarily and properly pre-empted by our business commitments and activities. But the establishment of a chaplaincy to cater for spiritual needs is a timely and very welcome addition to our overall infrastructure here at Canary Wharf and will, I know, be a source of help and inspirational guidance to many.
>
> (Sir David Walker, former Chairman, Barclays)

Canary Wharf Group and the Anglican Diocese of London had the imagination and foresight to establish a multifaith chaplaincy for the business community. Under Paul Reichmann's leadership, the Canadian company, Olympia and York, began the transformation of the disused docklands site in East London that led to today's familiar Canary Wharf estate. Paul Reichmann had trained as an Orthodox rabbi before he joined the family firm of property developers, and it is likely that his religious values influenced the humane design of the estate which, in conjunction with the office buildings, provides a congenial environment of waterside restaurants and cafes, parks, shops and transport links for the workers. During my interview for my job as chaplain, a senior executive of the

Canary Wharf Group stated that a chaplaincy was important to provide a spiritual element. He added that it was Canary Wharf Group's practice to close their construction sites and offices on the Jewish Sabbath and Jewish religious holidays, in addition to Christian ones. This practice continued until the company was sold to Songbird Estates in 2005. Another observation he made was that it was important for them that they were working with the Church of England as the established church to begin the process of building the chaplaincy.

In 2004, I set about establishing the chaplaincy. I was constrained by a number of factors, as Canary Wharf estate is a private business park owned by Canary Wharf Group. The owners made it clear from the outset that the chaplaincy was present on the estate as guest, was not to engage in proselytizing and had to work towards becoming multifaith. They were clear that in establishing the chaplaincy I needed to be mindful of the international, culturally diverse working community and therefore should be respectful of other people's lifestyles, cultures and beliefs.

The Anglican Diocese of London had its own expectations in sponsoring this new chaplaincy venture, primarily that it would be fully financially self-supporting within three years. It was also to fulfil the functions of bringing a faith presence into the world of work, provide pastoral care and support through personal or work-related issues, provide a forum to help facilitate engagement with critical spiritual, social and ethical questions which arise in the complexities of the working environment and provide a place and opportunities to share with individuals on their spiritual journeys.

In many ways, from the Church's perspective this is a standard formula of chaplaincy work as far as there is one. However, from my prior experience as a university chaplain, and in conversation with other sector chaplains, including hospital chaplains, I realized that establishing this new chaplaincy was far more complex than others I had encountered. I remember saying to the bishop at my interview that from my experience I anticipated it would take between seven to ten years for the chaplaincy to establish and become financially independent.

Over the first few weeks and months I faced a number of challenges. Previously as a university chaplain I had been used to an open-access environment model of chaplaincy, but in this context the high level of security in all office blocks made this impossible. In my first week I was in a lift and overheard two men speculating that if a suicide plane targeted Canary Wharf it would most likely hit the Barclays tower first, suggesting that after the 9/11 bombings in New York there was still a fear of working in high-rise buildings. This was confirmed one Sunday when I was sitting in a local church and the chap behind me leant forward and said, 'I know you, but you don't know me, and I watch you every day.' He went on to explain that he worked in the closed circuit TV control room at Canary Wharf, watching the monitors of all the surveillance cameras on the estate. Given this post-9/11 environment, and the London bombings of 7/7, it was clear that the chaplaincy needed to find a way of working in a place where high security was an everyday reality.

Working with global companies I faced another challenge. As I mentioned earlier, 'religion' or 'faith' was not immediately welcome in the workplace, and this was particularly true of non-UK companies. For example, when I met with the human resources director of an American law firm, she said she would keep my details on file, but they had no interest in offering chaplaincy to their employees, because as a US company this was not company policy. On another occasion, I had a 15-minute meeting with the diversity and inclusion director of a European bank, which I thought had gone well as we agreed to meet again in a few months' time, but the meeting did not happen for another two years! Fortunately, not all my initial encounters were so negative and unfriendly.

Most of the companies offer a vast array of personal support and benefits to their employees, such as counselling through their employee assistance programmes, occupational health, on-site health centres, and various other benefits. So the key challenges I faced were: what does the chaplaincy offer that complements the company's services, and how does chaplaincy fit within the company's structures?

These challenges continued, as every company has different structures, but after a while I realized that I was often being offered a way to build relationships. At the end of many conversations I would be asked, 'How can we as a company help you?' At first this surprised me because in most cases they had made it very clear that they were unable to support religion financially. Their question was crucial in encouraging me to rethink this ministry of chaplaincy for this context. It was not a case of 'doing things for people' or 'this is what the church or chaplaincy can offer you and your employees'. Instead, I came to realize that one of the key modes of working with companies was to explore how a partnership could be developed with them. Most basically this meant my asking for their help, whether it was to provide a meeting space and refreshments, or help with the design of appropriate posters, or advice with a human resources issue. Through these encounters I began to build relationships and mutual trust. In the early days it seemed to help with access that I was an Anglican priest under the authority of the Church of England as the established church. Maybe it was more about accountability and who was my line manager, but it certainly gave me credibility that I was part of a recognizable church. I will expand on this in more detail in a later chapter.

As I began to immerse myself in the place, I was also concerned not to lose a healthy critical awareness. Asking questions and listening carefully to the responses was crucial to understanding the business community. To help me do this I felt that it was important to at least have a fundamental working knowledge of economics. My own background so far had been science and theology. So through the Birkbeck Department of Continuing Education I enrolled on a three-month part-time course entitled 'Introduction to Economic Principles' delivered through the London School of Economics. The aim of doing this for me was to at least be able to ask intelligent questions and understand the answer enough to ask the next question. It was about understanding the language. I am always amazed how useless I find foreign language phrase books; I might be able to ask a question in a particular language, but I never understand the answer. I learnt enough of the language of economics and finance to help engage with my particular community.

I had assumed that my initial contact with the banks and law firms would be through human resources departments as this had been my former way of working as a university chaplain. In Canary Wharf it wasn't so straightforward. By a series of referrals, I eventually found myself having coffee with the head of diversity in one of the large banks. We began to meet regularly, and I learnt about the diversity issues and challenges within the bank and we explored together what I might offer as the chaplain. She then referred me to a colleague in another bank, where I could use my new-found knowledge to ask questions and learn even more. Then she in turn introduced me to a colleague in another bank, and so the process continued and relationships began to be built.

As trust grew so partnerships grew, and relationships have been further strengthened. A number of companies have now run joint events with the chaplaincy within their offices: panel discussions, seminars and roundtable discussions, all with a faith element. For example, the chaplains recently led a panel discussion around faith and finance in one of the companies, and we have been asked by other companies to offer similar events. These joint events have opened the way to raising the chaplaincy profile within their institutions and led to deeper conversations about how the chaplaincy's work of pastoral care and spiritual support complements their existing employee benefit and support programmes.

I mentioned earlier that a condition of the estate owners in supporting the establishing of the chaplaincy was that I had to work towards it becoming multifaith. It was only when the chaplaincy had won the trust of the companies that some became willing to support it financially, which then made it possible for me to appoint a Muslim and a Jewish chaplain to the team. Prior to this I had painstakingly demonstrated to the companies that the chaplaincy was for all employees, and not just Church of England. It was helpful that the Church of England has always understood its ministry as being defined as a geographical parish rather than a congregation of specific people who had chosen to attend or take up membership, and I tried to demonstrate that my role as chaplain followed the same principle of providing pastoral care and spiritual support to all who asked – individuals or teams.

However, for many non-UK companies this was a difficult concept to grasp. In many instances I was asked about specific chaplaincy provision for Muslims or Jews or people of other faiths or of no declared faith allegiance. I would try to explain that, if in conversation with someone it was evident that I was not the right person, I would refer the individual to another more suitable person or agency – a member of their own faith community, a counsellor, GP, or other adviser. But it was not enough to state this in principle; I needed to show it in practice. For example, in conversation with a young man it emerged that he felt he was in the wrong job, so we explored together who might best help him and I put him in touch with both a business coach and a careers adviser. On another occasion I had a conversation with a man distressed about his marriage and I helped him and his wife to be supported by their local vicar. In another situation, I gave continuing support to a Hindu woman who was in the process of leaving a violent marriage by ensuring that she was getting the right kind of assistance through other agencies.

To help companies further understand that I was available to all faiths and none, I began to distribute to all diversity and inclusion directors and offices an attractive printed faith calendar listing the dates of all the main faith holidays and festivals. While this information is readily available on the internet, for ease the local London Borough of Tower Hamlets[5] annually produces its own version and in recent years different companies have financed the printed version, and it is this I distribute.

Many chaplains in today's pluralistic society exercise a role as 'faith adviser'. Within Canary Wharf, this role has been entrusted to me by the managers with whom I have built strong relationships. The scope of this role has grown to include: advising employees who are moving to work in other countries and cultures; helping employees from other countries and cultures to settle within the UK; involvement in conversations about the role of faith groups in the workplace (a much-debated issue by employers – should they remain informal or be formalized?); advising on the management of prayer rooms and facilities; meeting with leaders of the informal company faith groups at the request of senior managers when there have been questions about what kind of faith events are appropriate within the workplace; and bereavement support.

A significant development of this work is that since 2009 I have co-chaired the Canary Wharf Diversity and Inclusion (D&I) Forum together with the D&I manager of American bank State Street. Recently, the other co-chair of the Forum has changed, it is now the D&I manager at Northern Trust. The forum is for all the D&I managers of the companies based in Canary Wharf. It meets twice a year and is the only one of the many D&I forums that includes faith among its discussions.

The chaplaincy has come a long way since it was first established, when I was told bluntly that companies did not 'do' religion. Most companies are now much more aware, appreciative and open to the role that faith can contribute to their workplaces. For example, in recent years, since the global financial crisis, companies within the financial sector have more actively engaged in improving their internal cultures and ensuring that their employees operate according to their espoused values and ethics. This has given chaplaincy many opportunities to explore the place of wisdom and how this can provide a dynamic exchange between faith and workplace practices for achieving the core business of the company. (I explore this particular issue in a later chapter.)

Another important factor in establishing and growing the work of the chaplaincy has been accountability. The relationship any chaplaincy has with its host institution in terms of accountability is complex, even more so given the complexity of Canary Wharf. A recent report of the Church of England's involvement in chaplaincy underlines this, stating that '[chaplaincies] are publicly recognized and validated by both the host organization/network and the faith community; and chaplains are appropriately accountable to both the host organization/network as well as to their faith community' (Church of England 2014).

The Canary Wharf Multifaith Chaplaincy is accountable in terms of its strategy, operating model and financial management to the estate owners, Canary Wharf Group, and to the office tenants via the Canary Wharf Chaplaincy Steering Group. The Canary Wharf Chaplaincy Steering Group comprises senior managers from a number of the global companies. In addition, each chaplain is accountable to his or her faith community, in my case to the Church of England Bishop of London.

Today, 13 years later, I have overcome the two biggest initial challenges: we are now a multifaith chaplaincy, and we are financially sustainable. A number of other factors have been essential as I have worked towards these goals; they have been to build the idea of legacy into the development of the chaplaincy from the beginning, creating a multifaith team that gathered individuals and crucially sustained networking, building on existing relationships and partnerships and continuing to look for new ones with the companies; and to instil within the team a continued process of reviewing services we offer and the challenges the business community faces to help us stay relevant to our context. Finally, not having a chaplaincy building might to some have been a significant disadvantage, but in this situation it has been a blessing, giving the chaplains freedom to build relationships by asking for help, to ask companies for space for meetings and events, to minister incarnationally and to be visible where people are.

Why faith and religion are important in the workplace

The Canary Wharf Multifaith Chaplaincy acts as a focal point and a conduit for faith and finance to connect in Canary Wharf.

(Alan Smith, Global Head of Risk
Strategy, HSBC Holdings Plc)

As mentioned earlier, when I began this chaplaincy most of the companies made it very clear that they did not do religion in the workplace, it was not appropriate. However, over time, within the business community of Canary Wharf the faith communities have increased in their visibility. The Muslim community, for example, continues to grow and is impacting on many companies, particularly as their holy day is Friday. The legacy from the original Jewish owners of the estate endures, with physical reminders during the year such as the Sukkot and the Menorah, and Christians are evident with their groups and activities. Sadly, it is often tragic events, whether global or local, that provide a reason for the chaplaincy to offer hospitality to the business community at large. After the 7/7 bombings in London, the chaplaincy brought the business community together for a multifaith event in response to the tragedies, and it also gathered the Hindu and Sikh business communities together after the Mumbai bombings. Most recently, the chaplaincy organized a multifaith event to commemorate the centenary of the beginning of the First World War on Armistice Day in 2014.

In the West we are discovering that religion is very much a part of the public sphere, in the world, in politics, conflicts of various sorts, and day-to-day relationships, including those in business. Previous assumptions that religion was on the decline particularly in the West and in communist countries have proved not to be the case. Religion plays a significant role within today's globalized world, and this is particularly true for the Middle East, Africa and Asia where it thrives alongside economic and technical advances. The Pew Research Center's Forum on Religion & Public Life estimated in 2010 that there were 5.8 billion religiously affiliated adults and children around the globe, representing 84 per cent of the world's population of 6.9 billion. Or to put it another way, worldwide more than eight in ten people identify with a religious group.

Within Canary Wharf there are offices that form part of larger global businesses, which extend into many countries and cultures throughout the world. Globalization has changed how the world relates; there are many complex relationships and blurred boundaries in terms of public and private interests and between the interests of a single nation state and those of the wider international community. In the light of the global financial crisis we have seen just how complicated it is for companies operating within different countries, cultures and religions.

We live in a world where religion can no longer be marginalized. David Ford, former Regius Professor of Divinity at Cambridge University, in a speech he made in October 2013 at a dinner at Mansion House, City of London, said:

> Religion is one of the world's key challenges, both locally and globally... It is no longer viable to 'not do God'...

> We're not good at talking about religion in the UK and yet it's crucial for our communities and businesses to be more religiously literate in a globalized society.

I suggest that businesses can no longer ignore the place of religion within their organizations, given the diversity of the workforce and the different countries in which many companies now operate. At times religion will play a direct role in business decisions, for example opening an office in the Middle East, such as Saudi Arabia, is fraught with many challenges, not least ensuring that the company's working practices do not fall foul of the country's religious laws. Expectations as to what is acceptable or 'normal' will differ. For example, in Saudi Arabia, issues around gender contradict Western norms of gender equality. In Canary Wharf, companies have global workforces that embrace people of different nationalities, cultures, religions and lifestyles. This not only provides for enormous creativity and learning but also for potential conflict, so it is therefore important to make space for dialogue. Professor David Ford is often to be heard saying that 'we need to improve the quality of our disagreements', particularly in the context of interfaith dialogue, and that in disagreeing with each other, we also learn from each other and have integrity where we differ. I think this is sound advice for other contexts, including working with the entire diverse workforce, not just between people of faith.

The reality is that as individuals and businesses we need to appreciate that we live and work within a world that is both multifaith and secular and we must find ways to embrace both, not allowing secular world views and principles to monopolize the public sphere in the name of neutrality. It is important that we find ways of forming the sort of mutual ground that allows each tradition to contribute from its core belief, understanding and practice. A way to achieve this is through using wisdom. This concept of wisdom is a common theme in a number of different faith traditions, although it is not exclusive to religion. Wisdom, and in particular literature about wisdom, can help to shape understanding and engagement with issues and challenges in contemporary life. People of different faith traditions are able to contribute their valuable wisdom from their faiths and help bridge the gap in the workplace between multifaith and secular worlds.

The chaplaincy has been involved in several initiatives bringing together workers to learn from one another and share wisdom from their faith traditions. In one of the banks it helped set up a forum of representatives of different faiths, to provide space for members to listen and learn from each other. It discovered a further role: to give feedback to the employer on how the company can best help people of faith to perform to their full potential in the workplace; for example, providing adequate prayer room facilities, catering for dietary requirements in the restaurant and supporting various work-related faith events. On another occasion I chaired a panel of senior bankers, including a Muslim, a Jew and a Christian. The topic for discussion was how people of faith could work within the financial services with integrity and contribute to the core business. On another occasion the chaplaincy was consulted about how to prepare non-Muslim colleagues for their attendance at the funeral of a Muslim colleague. As a chaplain, I have discovered that when people are encouraged to bring their whole selves to work, including their faith, this enables them to be totally present in each task they do. When human beings are functioning in every area of their lives – intellectual, emotional, moral and spiritual – then they are able to fully participate in the discussion, decisions and actions and mirror the values and ethical standards espoused by their business community.

Many decisions made in business are complex; they do not have black and white solutions. Decisions need to be made and people have to take responsibility for them. In the main, a decision can only be made using the information available at the time, trying to consider the implications of a decision and trying to do the right thing. Hindsight is a wonderful thing and there will be times that with hindsight a different decision might have been made. However, when we make decisions we do not have the benefit of hindsight until it's too late. It is important to ensure that all decision making is informed by a good process, with all the available information and tools to make the best decision possible. For some this will include the principles of their faith.

For people of faith to be fully functioning they need to be able to integrate their faith and their work lives. Crucial to this is to help them to gain a more adult and mature understanding of their own faith and how it might assist them to navigate through complex situations and decision making. Often a person's faith can be undeveloped, lacking experience or theological understanding to cope with ambiguity, leading to a tendency to offer on occasion judgemental or naive comments or to disengage their brain from their faith. They need help to think theologically in as wise a way as possible, rather than trying to operate with a range of 'packaged' ethics. Each challenge will be different and its particularities need to be taken into account in making moral judgements.

As a chaplaincy we welcome the opportunity to encourage and engage with people of faith to help them build on the foundations of their own faith for moral and ethical living. For some it might be advantageous to understand the history of economic development within their faith, and how their faith tradition has evolved in its understanding of various practices around money, wealth, purpose and value of work and social responsibility.

One practical way my colleagues and I have helped our particular faith communities is by either offering courses or participating in ones already taking place. For example, my Jewish colleague regularly contributes to the Jewish business community's established programme of 'Lunch and Learns'.[6]

My Muslim colleague has designed Khatib[7] training for Muslims in the business community. In partnership with other organizations I have developed a programme called the 'Faith & Work Forum' for middle to senior Christian managers. I will expand on these in a later chapter.

The need of the business world to listen to the world and local communities

Lord Adair Turner said in his Mansion House speech in 2009 that:

> Some financial activities which proliferated over the last 10 years were 'socially useless'…and if you disagree with that, you have a bone to pick not only with me but with the chairman of the British Bankers Association, Stephen Green, who has said exactly the same thing in similar words, when he argued that 'in recent years, banks have chased short-term profits by introducing complex products of no real use to humanity'.
>
> (Turner 2009)

At the height of the credit crunch this was quite an indictment and much criticism was laid at the door of the bankers. They had lost the trust of the general public, their customers and governments. They were accused of no longer acting in a way that contributed to the common good. With a number of protests around the world, the heads of the financial institutions were forced to listen and governments began to challenge their operations and impose stricter regulation. It is important to stress that not all banking services were failing to provide appropriate services. Often I would find myself reminding people outside the banks that not everyone who worked in a bank was a banker and that people worked in other areas such as facilities management, human resources, IT and so on.

In a small way, chaplaincy was able to facilitate conversations with the local community, in addition to facilitating conversations with corporate social responsibility managers as well as the leaders of these institutions. One of the things I set up in partnership with Morgan Stanley and later with HSBC was a training day for ordinands (trainee Church of England vicars and chaplains) which provided an insight into the world of banking, including the mistakes leading to the credit crunch and the cultural nature of the workplace and its challenges, and was an opportunity for critical and honest dialogue with bankers and a section of the community that they would not normally come into contact with. From a church perspective, it provided the chance for the ordinands to understand the context of some of the people they might be ministering to once they became vicars. Among the ordinands' feedback I have had comments such as: 'I have a better understanding of the complexity of the workforce and the issues they face' and 'I discovered that there are distinctive and different work cultures even within one industry' and 'I will continue to reflect on the ethics of business, work priorities, and the identity and nature of money'. These partnerships have also helped the business people to explore their working environments from other viewpoints.

More recent examples of this include a follow-up to a conference in May 2015 on the G30 Report *Banking Conduct and Culture: A Call for Sustained and Comprehensive Reform*, hosted by Queen Mary University of London Centre for Commercial Law Studies, Institute for Regulation and Ethics. To my amazement, when I suggested to the group of people from companies based in Canary Wharf who participated at the conference that we continue to meet, they all agreed. I was then involved in facilitating the group to explore ways of sharing some of the good practice, and this process will continue until autumn 2017 when it is hoped that the group will produce a helpful booklet. In another example, one of the banks hosted a round-table conversation with members of the Banking Standards Board and senior executives from several companies who were people of faith to discuss the role of faith in conduct and culture within financial services.

There have also been opportunities to bring in church leaders and a group of rabbis to meet with people who work in the financial sector, whether they were bankers, lawyers or regulators, and have serious and straightforward conversations. These were not opportunities for 'banker bashing' but aimed to provide understanding of the complexities, particularly of the credit crunch, while retaining a critical overview.

As a chaplain I have found it important to maintain and be involved in local community networks outside Canary Wharf, which have included local Church of England clergy groups and churches, ecumenical church groups and interfaith groups, to help build bridges across the two diverse communities of Canary Wharf and the London Borough of Tower Hamlets. At the outset when I first began establishing the chaplaincy there was still a lot of hurt and resentment in the local community that the docks had been closed in the 1980s. From the start of the original regeneration planning for Canary Wharf, the local community, faith groups, voluntary groups and others had opposed the building of this wealthy looking financial centre on the basis that they felt that local people would not benefit from it. The local borough is one of the poorest boroughs in the country.

One of the ways I began to build bridges into the community was to visit and preach in most of the local Church of England churches and offer to do cover during clergy holidays or during interregnums. In conversations with some of the local people I realized that they couldn't understand why these 'wealthy people' in Canary Wharf needed a chaplain. Not long after I had been chaplain I had two pastoral assistants who lived and worshipped in Tower Hamlets come to Canary Wharf on a short placement. They were both sceptical of Canary Wharf as a financial district and could not understand why the people who worked there needed a chaplain; surely God has sent us to the poor and needy? When I came to read their placement reports, one of them said they now understood why these people too needed a chaplain, 'Jesus said blessed are the poor in spirit', and the pastoral assistant had been very aware of the people's spiritual poverty.

The challenges that have been facing the financial sector since the credit crunch have been related to restoring trust, especially among the general public, and changing the banking culture. While this was probably the worst failure in banking in living memory, at the time of writing this book, it was not the first and it will not be the last. However, important lessons are being learned including revisiting values, ethics and behaviour that are appropriate in this world.

Crucial to the success of establishing this particular workplace chaplaincy has been to ensure and work towards it being a multifaith chaplaincy. In the next chapter I will discuss this in more detail.

3

Multifaith Chaplaincy

Globalization, faith and economic activity

The World Economic Forum has recognized that religion, far from diminishing in the world, is still very much a part of people's lives worldwide. The forum comments that:

> with 80% of the world's population adhering to a religion, faith communities represent a powerful driver for transformation and change. The World Economic Forum recognizes the relevance of religion and faith to the global economy, politics, society and individuals, and is keenly aware of the important role played by faith communities around the world in advancing human society in an inclusive and sustainable way.
>
> (World Economic Forum 2015)

In this chapter, I continue the argument that a chaplaincy can play a positive role within the workplace given that in the majority of the world, faith and religion are influential factors in people's daily and work lives. However, although Christianity is still the majority religion in the UK, there are distinct advantages in chaplaincy in the workplace being genuinely multifaith.

The globalization of economic activity has become well established over the last 30 years or so. Even in its infancy there was much discussion by economists, scientists, academics, politicians and the media about the effect of economic globalization. It is interesting to note that even in the early days as global economic activity grew there were consultations about the role of faith in the growing global business activity. In 1984, under the patronage of HRH Prince Philip, Duke of Edinburgh, and HRH Crown Prince El Hassan bin Talal of Jordan a group was convened of distinguished members of the three Abrahamic faiths to deliberate on topics of common interest.

The aim of the consultations was to discuss an interfaith code of ethics for international business, formulated in the light of the religious traditions of the three monotheistic faiths. These discussions were concluded in October 1993 in Amman. The provisions of the guidelines reflect the ethical bases indicated in the teaching of the three religions. Those involved in the process agreed a declaration based on a shared concern for justice, mutual respect, stewardship and honesty. It illustrated in a practical way that people of very different cultures or beliefs have more in common than is sometimes apparent. They hoped that the sense of this interfaith declaration would be 'incorporated into Statements of Purpose or Codes to Conduct. It is offered on the understanding that it will help facilitate expanding international economic activity, which is beneficial for harmonious international relations and prosperity' (Webley 1993, p.6).

This early initiative exploring the role of faith in business certainly suggests that there is a place for chaplaincy and multifaith chaplaincy given that 80 per cent of the world's population adhere to a religion. Due to the international nature of the workforce within Canary Wharf, it is like working within a mini United Nations.

Diverse and integrated society and workforce

With global trade comes global movement of the workforce. As companies operate in many parts of the world, with this come opportunities for employees to move around the world while continuing to work for the same company. This may be in the form of just an inter-country transfer or it may be part of the management training scheme. In London, as in other large cities around the world, the workforce is international, multicultural and diverse. It is important to remember that the workforce is not just diverse through global movement within companies, but that increasingly our societies have become more integrated through immigration, as other cultural and faith communities contribute to the life of a diverse nation as a whole. This has a direct impact when we begin to explore what this means in terms of religion and faith adherence. Table 3.1 show the breakdown of faith as shown by the 2001 and 2011 censuses for England and Wales (Office of National Statistics 2001, 2011).

Table 3.1 Breakdown of faith from the 2001 and 2011 censuses for England and Wales

	England and Wales		London	
	2001	2011	2001	2011
Christians	71.8	59.3	58.0	48.4
Muslims	2.8	4.9	8.5	12.4
Hindus	1.0	1.5	4.1	5.0
Sikhs	0.6	0.8		1.5
Jews	0.5	0.5	2.1	1.8
Buddhists	0.3	0.4	0.8	1.0
Others	0.3	0.4	0.5 (Sikhs included here)	0.6

The 2011 census for Scotland shows a similar trend for the two largest faith groups: 53.8 per cent Christian and 1.4 per cent Muslim (Scottish Office of National Statistics 2011). As one might expect, the picture for London, given the international and multicultural population, shows a slightly higher population for minority faith communities compared with the remainder of the UK. This has a direct impact on the work and formation of a chaplaincy team working particularly in large companies that reflect this diversity.

A number of the global banks have a workforce based in Canary Wharf (as well as the City of London and other cities within the UK), but their parent company is located in America. Given the large number of American companies that have offices based in the UK, it is of interest to reflect briefly on the scene in the USA. Worldwide, the fastest growing overarching perspective on life is not secular humanism but religion. The fastest growing religions today are Islam and Christianity. Christianity is now growing much faster in the non-Western parts of the globe. According to the Pew Research Center (2015), the breakdown of religions in the USA is similar to the UK, with Christianity the largest group at 70 per cent, then Judaism 1.9 per cent and Islam 0.9 per cent, Hinduism and Buddhism both at 0.7 per cent. In the UK, the Muslim community is still relatively small, but it is the largest faith community after Christianity. The Croatian–American theologian Miroslav Volf makes an observation about the workplace growing in significance with regard to religious plurality. From an American perspective he writes, 'In terms of religious diversity, it is a nearly exact though somewhat smaller replica of the wider culture' (Volf 2011, p.122). This is also true for London and other large cities in the UK.

In the USA and in the UK, religion in the workplace has become a significant issue. Indeed, within the UK, under the Equality and Human Rights Commission, religion is included alongside, race, gender, disability, age, sexual orientation and transgender. In New York there is an organization called 'Tanenbaum',[8] which is a secular organization focusing on interreligious dialogue, helping to combat religious prejudice in a number of areas, including the workplace.

The diversity and inclusion agenda is now an important part of the workplace. Diversity means a respect for and appreciation of differences, especially within the following groups: ethnicity, gender, age, national origin, disability, sexual orientation and religion. But diversity must also be about inclusion, acknowledging the contribution people make from their diverse perspectives, work experiences, lifestyles and cultures, where each individual is valued, respected and supported, enabling them to achieve their full potential. All companies want to ensure that this is deeply embedded within their culture and practices and their relationships with both employees and customers or clients.

A direct consequence of this agenda in terms of the religion or faith strand is to ensure that there are contemplation or quiet rooms, prayer rooms for the faith groups and individuals to use during the working day. Another one is the increasing celebration of faith festivals within the company and the understanding and importance of these in the life of a particular faith community. So, for example, this includes Jewish Chanukah and Muslim Eid parties alongside the Christian carol service.

In the rest of the globe, religion has always played a significant role in economic life. In a previous chapter, I mentioned the issues around setting up an office in the Middle East and the importance of understanding the local religious laws and rules.

In the last few years I have come across examples of prayer rooms being set up in different parts of the world other than airports. In 2012, the first Muslim prayer room was set up in a Japanese shopping mall as increasing numbers of tourists visit from Malaysia. I have also seen a Malaysian tourist website which now refers to prayer rooms in shopping malls. If one googles shopping mall and prayer rooms, they are now all over the world, including the mainly Buddhist country Thailand.

I have also come across articles about how devoutly religious people make better workers. An interesting article appeared in the BBC news (2010) referring to a growing number of businesses run by Christian entrepreneurs in one of China's key enterprise zones; so great has been the economic success that the Chinese government is studying it. More recently, an article from the BBC news (2015) gives two examples: one of a Chinese Christian businessman who believes that his Christian values have helped make his firm more profitable, and a Chinese Buddhist businessman who draws on his Buddhist teachings to help underpin his company's culture.

Workplace chaplaincy

Multifaith chaplaincy is well established in healthcare, universities, prisons and in the armed services where the chaplaincies work within the structures of their particular institutions. The Canary Wharf Chaplaincy is purposefully a multifaith chaplaincy in the workplace for both individuals and companies. It is unique and has developed a particular ethos and style for working for this context. There is one other similar model that I am aware of, which is the Greenwich Peninsula Chaplaincy, where chaplains and volunteers from various faith groups are available for chats in the multifaith prayer space.

While workplace chaplaincy is a growing sector across the UK, it continues to remain distinctly Christian, and there is a reluctance to incorporate other faith leaders within the teams. I think there are a number of reasons for this. Often workplace chaplaincy is a local initiative, coming from an ecumenical group of Christians; an example of this would be volunteers offering chaplaincy to shops in the high street or retail malls. Town centre Church of England churches have been at the forefront, often working with other Christian denominations to set up town centre chaplaincies for the various business people and businesses located within the town. In 2013 the Alliance of Town and City Chaplaincies was set up to link and provide support for the town and city chaplaincies, and chaplaincies wishing the join this network must be 'distinctively' Christian. If one carries out a Google search on the internet, workplace chaplaincies will describe themselves as Christian. It has been suggested (Ryan 2015) that given the ascendance of the evangelical wing of the Church of England, it follows that more of our town centre clergy and chaplains will be evangelicals, who often are less enthusiastic to engage in multifaith chaplaincy.

I think it is easier for these chaplaincies to be exclusively Christian if their aim is to provide opportunities and events for business people to come to, rather than engage directly with building relationships with companies. This gives them more freedom than working directly with companies who have a strong ethos in terms of a diversity and inclusion agenda, where they might feel constrained by the expectation that they must respect without criticism other people's lifestyles, cultures and beliefs.

This Christian nature of workplace chaplaincy is not just a UK phenomenon; it is also true in the USA. For example, Marketplace Ministries, which advertises itself as 'the world's original and leading workplace chaplaincy provider', provides corporate chaplains who are contracted or hired by a company. Initially there is little specific Christian language, but if one digs deeper into the website then one discovers that the organization appears to have an exclusively Christian overarching aim which is about converting people to Christianity.[9] Interestingly, it has now extended its work to the UK, and its Christian nature and intentions are more explicit.[10] Clearly Marketplace Ministries is valued by various workplaces within the USA. Yet my initial experience of working with large American global companies was very different. In Canary Wharf, the companies, and American companies in particular, were unhappy with an exclusively Christian chaplaincy, and all were very clear that I was to refrain from proselytizing. The first question I would often get asked was, 'What about other faiths and those of no faith?'

What difference does it make if chaplaincy is multifaith?

In operating a chaplaincy in the workplace, particularly where there is a very diverse multicultural workforce, it is becoming less acceptable to offer chaplaincy from a purely Christian perspective. In the same way that prison or healthcare chaplaincies have had to embrace multifaith chaplaincy, so too will workplace chaplaincy in the future or there is a possibility that chaplaincies will no longer be welcome if they continue to be Christian. As I write this I can hear many of the objections from chaplaincies which feel that their Christian identity is imperative.

I am aware too that there are Christians working on the Canary Wharf estate who are unhappy about the multifaith nature of our chaplaincy. In 2014 the chaplaincy underwent a radical rebranding of its entire publicity. It was reported to me that since the rebranding someone had stopped attending the weekly Christian lunchtime service as she disapproved of the 'new' multifaith status of the chaplaincy, although it had been an open part of our publicity for the previous three years or so. I was disappointed that this person had not come to discuss her concerns with me. My guess is that she will not be the only one who is unhappy, but I believe the pros far outweigh the cons in operating a multifaith chaplaincy.

However, a surprising and unexpected consequence of setting up a multifaith chaplaincy is that it has enabled each chaplain to hold on to the integrity of their own faith without compromising their faith tradition. Once I had appointed both a Jewish and a Muslim colleague, I discovered that I was given much more freedom to express views from a Christian perspective, and therefore no longer needed to have a much more measured approach in trying to ensure that I was always inclusive and mentioned other faiths. As faith is on the increase in the public arena, my chaplaincy colleagues and I are in a privileged position to be involved in debates and conversations, particularly within the workplace where people spend a large part of their week.

In terms of credibility, it has been crucial for the multifaith chaplaincy to embody the positive aspects of faith in the workplace. Given that most people who work for global companies are working in very diverse teams, of different nationalities, cultures, faiths and lifestyles, a multifaith chaplaincy too needs to function well as a team, rather than acting as a loose group of individuals. This means that we have to work at being a team and try to resolve issues that might cause tensions. The focus of our team is that together we are providing chaplaincy services to the business community in Canary Wharf drawing on shared expertise in our respective faith traditions.

In developing a multifaith team it has been important to recognize that each chaplain will bring different skills and talents as well as knowledge in their own faith tradition. It is right that they use their own expertise and minister to their own faith groups. For example, my Catholic colleague is the only member of the team who can preside at a Catholic Mass and my Muslim colleague is the only one who can lead Friday prayers. There are particularities within each faith that only their faith leader can help with or support people from those faiths with, and it is important to recognize and support this.

However, for a multifaith team to function well and engage with the business world, members of the team need to be able to work together on projects, be willing to be the first point of contact for anyone approaching the chaplaincy and then refer to another member of the team as required. I have discovered that since my other faith colleagues joined the team we have been asked to take part in more events or suggest events where members of the team can be seen working together. The huge advantage of working with a multifaith chaplaincy is that companies are willing to engage with the chaplaincy in matters related to faith in the workplace. For our part we ensure that we provide events that are business focused, supporting people of faith or no faith, and we are respectful of companies' diversity and inclusion policies.

In building and developing the team, I have had to reflect deeply on how we bring our own spiritual lives to bear on the chaplaincy and one another. When I was a university chaplain and led a team of only Christian chaplains, we prayed regularly together. However, I did not feel comfortable using formal audible prayers as a multifaith team, so we begin our team meetings with shared silence, which we find very powerful. It enables each chaplain to pray within their own tradition without having to agree or disagree with the format or words of a prayer that is different from their own faith. We are clear that we belong to different faith communities, but we work hard at finding common ground in the focus of our work as chaplains. Quite often we engage as a team or with another chaplain in theological reflection, maybe related to an issue or a circumstance that we have been asked about. As a team we have been asked how companies might respond to various terrorist attacks around the world in supporting their employees. For example, it was helpful for us to discuss as a team the issues relating to the attacked on the *Charlie Hebdo* offices in Paris in 2015 and why for many Muslims the publication of cartoons depicting the Prophet Muhammed was highly offensive.

In an interview I was asked about the theology of our chaplaincy. My response was that we would probably have as many theologies as there are chaplains. I think actually we live out our theology every time we have to grapple with an issue that might cause tension within the team, or every time we do an event together and discuss how we do it. In terms of multifaith chaplaincy, the theology of what we are about is organic and continues to grow and change with time.

I want to give an example of how we as a team have functioned together and worked out how we remain true to our own faith traditions. In November 2014 the team was ask to help organize and lead a multifaith commemoration for the start of the First World War. We chose not refer to it as a service but an event, so that each chaplain was free to make an appropriate contribution from their own faith. It did not mean that we could not mention God – quite the contrary – but God was spoken about from each tradition rather than as just a common denominator, which would have left the event bland and possibly meaningless for those people of faith who attended.

Sometimes in the world of trying to be inclusive in the workplace, the bias is often in favour of those who say that they are not religious so they are not offended. However, in doing this, inevitably people of faith can feel marginalized. As I mentioned earlier, within an international workforce it is important to recognize that people of faith want to be included too. There are times when it is important to be biased in favour of people of faith. For example, there are occasions when I am asked to help a company plan a memorial service or a service of thanksgiving for a colleague who has died. In each instance, I will help the people involved to plan the event, such as deciding on the number of readings and their length, the number of pieces of music and suitability, how many eulogies and their length and how the room should be set up. At that point my style is to hand the event over to the planning team to lead the event, and normally up to this point God or religion has not been mentioned. However, if they then ask me to lead the service, I do so on condition I mention

God at some point in a gentle, non-threatening way, as it is important for those people attending who have a faith for it to be recognized.

The chaplaincy is often contacted following the death of a colleague. Again, it is helpful to have a multifaith team. There was one occasion when my Muslim colleague and I worked together to help a particular company. The colleague who had died was Muslim and he was going to have a Muslim funeral. Many of the colleagues wanting to attend the funeral had never been to a Muslim funeral before, and so together we were able to prepare them. In particular, my colleague explained what they might expect to happen both in the mosque and at the graveside, and the level of participation possible for non-Muslim male and female colleagues. He explained, for example, that only the men would be allowed into the mosque for the funeral, that while the men and women would be able to go to the graveside they would have to keep their distance. We also explained the support we could offer grieving colleagues, such as a listening ear over a coffee, as well as offering space within the workplace for people to remember their colleague who for whatever reason were unable to attend the funeral.

Another issue we often meet is that of interfaith marriage. There have been a number of occasions where we as colleagues have discussed an issue that has arisen as result of a member of one faith community who has married someone from another faith community. Everything is fine until the first child arrives, and then the tensions begin between the couple – in whose faith will the child be raised?

As a multifaith team we provide much more than pastoral care or spiritual support. Within an internationally diverse workforce many people hold deep religious convictions, so it is beneficial to encourage people of faith to integrate their faith and work lives, and for everyone to grow in religious literacy. As we continue to live in a society where individual faith adherence is on the decrease but faith in the public arena is on the increase, religious literacy has become an important issue. Indeed, there is an initiative by the organization Coexist[11] to provide religious literacy programmes. Its partners include Ernst & Young, the Foreign and Commonwealth Office and the BBC, to name but a few.

Christianity, Judaism and Islam have long traditions of wisdom literature, which over centuries has influenced their societies' values, ethics and way of life. As part of a multifaith chaplaincy, my colleagues and I are able to help people of faith draw on their own traditions of wisdom and make a contribution with others to bring wisdom into the workplace. I will explore this further in the following chapter.

In building a multifaith chaplaincy team it is important to be realistic about the faiths included and how much chaplaincy time is required. According to the last census figures for London, Christianity is still the dominant faith, followed by Islam. It therefore made sense for me to appoint an imam. Within the financial and professional services there is a relatively sizable community of Jews and so it was sensible to appoint a Jewish chaplain. In Canary Wharf there is still a legacy from the original owners of the estate who were Orthodox Jews, so it was therefore appropriate to ensure that an Orthodox rabbi was appointed. Given the specific faith needs of Catholic Christians, it was also important to appoint a Catholic chaplain. According to the last census there is a larger faith community of Hindus than Jews – this is I think reflected within Canary Wharf which has a large Hindu working population. I am in the process of exploring the best way to provide chaplaincy for them as their needs are very different from the groups described so far. In the meantime, I have discovered that Hindus are very happy to chat to chaplains from other faith traditions, and a number have sought me out.

It is important to be realistic rather than try to cover every faith for the sake of it. I can remember as a university chaplain always being asked why we did not have a Jewish student society. The perceived wisdom was that the university should have one given all the faith groups. In reality, the university did not have one because only a few Jewish students were studying there. As the chaplaincy grows, we will explore the needs of other faith communities and either appoint chaplains or ensure that we have good referral networks.

One of the important features at the Canary Wharf Multifaith Chaplaincy is its visibility. Indeed, my Muslim and Jewish colleagues are often spotted walking around the estate together. It is not only important to be seen, it is also important that we are easily identified as faith leaders from our own particular faiths. What chaplains wear is therefore important. My Catholic colleague and I as an Anglican priest both wear clerical collars, making us easily visible as Christian ministers. Interestingly, when we interviewed for our first Muslim chaplain most of the candidates shortlisted wore a suit with a shirt and tie. As an interview panel we had a conversation about how acceptable it would be to the business community to have an imam who wore cultural dress. As it turned out the candidate who wore cultural dress was the one most suited for the role of Muslim chaplain in Canary Wharf, and we have discovered that his cultural dress has not been a hindrance but a positive help in terms of his visibility to the community.

I think it might be helpful here to mention why we call ourselves a multifaith chaplaincy rather than an interfaith chaplaincy. We find it helpful to talk about a 'multifaith' chaplaincy as it reflects more accurately that we are a team comprising of different faith leaders who all come with expertise and knowledge of their own faith (rather than a team of generalists who might have trained as interfaith chaplains). Having chaplains who are specialists in their faith is helpful when working with companies and offers a value added element which is the strength of a multifaith team.

For us, the term 'interfaith' signifies how we work together, for example in interfaith dialogue or interfaith panel discussions.

I asked my Jewish and Muslim colleagues why they thought multifaith chaplaincy is important in the Canary Wharf context. Here are their responses:

> The Multifaith Chaplaincy at Canary Wharf sets an example to all of the companies at Canary Wharf, and beyond: diversity is not just a reality, it is a force for good. Multifaith chaplaincy works so well, not despite our differences, but because of them.
>
> (Rabbi Dr Moshe Freedman)

> Canary Wharf is a dynamic community of people from all walks of life. Many of them have a religious or faith background. Coming to work in Canary Wharf may sometimes create unnecessary pressure on some of them to leave their religious or faith identity at the door. The presence of the Canary Wharf Multifaith Chaplaincy and its services is therefore vital, especially for those who wish to be their whole self in their workplace and not have to leave behind what is a significant and crucial part of who they are.
>
> (Shaykh Ibrahim Mogra)

The Church of England (Anglicanism) and multifaith chaplaincy

There is often some criticism levelled about the role of the established Church of England within chaplaincy. I think this is possibly because it is viewed as having certain privileges that other churches or faiths do not have. But what is often forgotten is that with these privileges come responsibilities that other churches or faiths do not have.

At a multifaith reception in 2012, Queen Elizabeth II (head of the Church of England) made the following comments:

'The concept of our established church is occasionally misunderstood and I believe, commonly under-appreciated… its role is not to defend Anglicanism to the exclusion of other religions… Instead, the church has a duty to protect the free practice of all faiths in this country' (*The Guardian* 2012).

In terms of the Church of England remaining established, Lord Jonathan Sacks, former Chief Rabbi, has said that 'the established church keeps religion at the forefront of the nation'. In his 1990 Reith Lectures he advocated that in an age of pluralism and division, the established church was needed more than ever as its existence expressed a desire and fulfilled a need for shared values and the appreciation of faith (*The Telegraph* 2015).

This is also the view of the Muslim community. My colleague Shaykh Ibrahim Mogra says,

> As a person with a religious belief, I like the fact that we have an established church in the UK, which means our country is not exclusively a secular one. For me, it is as simple as having a significant presence of an 'official' religion, albeit Christianity, than none at all. This long historic tradition of having the Church of England as the established church whose supreme governor is also the monarch is welcomed by the majority of all the diverse religious and faith groups represented in the UK. I have often ended up defending the established church, even against some Christian groups calling for disestablishment. It has also been argued that it is discriminatory, for example, not to have imams in the House of Lords, and so, by removing the bishops and dis-establishing the Church, all religions and faiths would be equal. I don't believe dis-establishment is necessary nor the removal of bishops is the answer to create equality.
>
> The answer is the inclusion of the other religious and faith traditions of the UK in the House of Lords

while retaining the established church. In any case, I believe the Church of England bishops have brought not just the teachings of Christianity but also those of other religions and faiths into the debates and discussions. I'm confident that the bishops would adequately and robustly represent the views and needs of Muslim communities in the UK as and when required to do so. We have lines of communications with them and have developed personal friendships through inter-faith engagement and collaboration. I am personally consulted by a number of them from time to time.[12]

Many faith leaders have said that they welcome the unique role occupied by the Church of England, in that when occasions demand they can ensure that other faiths and other Christians bear public witness to the truth, justice and service which are needed at the heart of national life. An example of this can be seen in the report *Faithful Cities: A Call for Celebration, Vision and Justice* (Church of England 2006); although the Commission's origins were in the Church of England, its membership was broadened as a recognition of how urban contexts are now diverse in culture, ethnicity and faith.

As I have previously mentioned, the Church of England as the established church has been an important factor in setting up the Canary Wharf Multifaith Chaplaincy. Canary Wharf Group and the Diocese of London on behalf of the Church of England collaborated to bring about the chaplaincy. There are a number of strands associated with this, including, as some commented, that it was very clear as far as the businesses were concerned where to complain if they were unhappy with the way I provided chaplaincy.

Within this section, I intend to give a brief summary of the contribution made by the Church of England as the established church and how its ethos has continued to shape the work of the chaplaincy. It should be noted that while other churches and other faiths share a commitment to the work of chaplaincy, the Church of England as the established church sees it as an obligation because of its special concern for the national wellbeing and its partnership in every avenue of national life (Turnbull and McFadyen 2012, p.22). The Church of England is the established church, which is not the same as a state church like the continental Lutheran churches. In many European countries, churches receive money from the government to maintain their buildings, but this is not the case in the Church of England. Since the Reformation in the sixteenth century, the authority of the Pope has been replaced by the reigning monarch as head of the Church of England, hence linking church and state. Prior to the founding of the welfare state, i.e. social services, the Church of England tried to maintain a comprehensive provision of pastoral care through the parish system. The notion was that it provided a visible Christian presence in all residential areas in England that seek to provide spiritual care to all who live there, people of all faiths and none, not just to signed up members of the church. The Church also pioneered universal education until the growth of secularism and pluralism. Within the last 150 years or so Christian values were universally regarded as undergirding public life, with justice and social reform as an important part of its voice within the public arena, which they continue to be.

Since the Reformation, the Church of England has always seen itself with responsibilities towards the whole nation. Indeed, in recent times as other Christian denominations have closed or retreated especially from rural communities, the Church of England has stayed. The former Archbishop of Canterbury William Temple (1881–1944) underlines the responsibility of the Church of England in that he is alleged to have said, 'the Christian Church (Church of England) is the only co-operative society that exists for the benefit of its non-members' (Bunting 1996, p.238). The parish principle exercised by the Church of England means that it is committed to people both in the communities where people live and in the multiple communities that people belong to through shared interests or values.

My training and early ministerial experiences have shaped the way I minister as an Anglican priest. As a curate I learnt to engage and welcome everyone within the community, even if they did not come into the church. Nobody was ever turned away from the church because they did not fit. We also had to learn to live with disagreement over the ordination of women[13] (there were those who found it hard to accept my ministry as a woman priest).

I give this as background to help understand how as a priest in the established Church of England I used it as a model to build the Multifaith Chaplaincy in Canary Wharf and why it is effective. Church of England clergy have it in their DNA to minister to all, not just Anglicans, not just Christians and not even just people who say they have a faith, but to everyone who asks for help or wants to chat within their parish. By law, Church of England clergy are required to perform weddings or funerals for anyone who lives within their parish, should they request it, regardless of whether the person goes to church or not. This is not true for other Christian denominations or faith groups. This was and continues to be my model as a chaplain – a willingness to care for and support all who ask.

Often Catholic or faith chaplains will only minister to their own. Let's use the 2011 Census for London as a typical make-up of a work community: 48 per cent Christian, 12 per cent Muslim, 5 per cent Hindu, 2 per cent Sikh, 2 per cent Jewish, 0.5 per cent Buddhist and 32 per cent not religious. In most multifaith chaplaincies it is usually the Church of England chaplain (assisted by the other Christian chaplains such as Methodist, Baptist or United Reformed if present within the team) who minister to the main bulk of the community (both Christian and of no religion). So if at Canary Wharf we operated this model, then I would be ministering to nearly 75 per cent of the working community! However, within chaplaincy there needs to be an openness to minister to all, those of faith and those who say they have no religious conviction. This is the model I have been trying to foster.

The Church of England has often been referred to as a 'broad church', as over the years it has tried to be balanced and avoid theological extremes, holding within it a variation of views in a respectful and generous way. At the heart of the Church of England (Anglicanism in general) is a dialogue model for resolving differences through conversation, slowly reflecting on issues that have potential both to divide and unite. Martin Percy (2013, p.20) has given us a timely reminder, 'Anglicanism is a community of being, love, thought and worship, rather than being a definitive body that has achieved mutually agreeable confessional closure.' The breadth of Anglicanism enables people of differing theological views to exist together, rather than excluding people because they do not hold to one accepted viewpoint. This too is a good undergirding principle of people of different faiths trying to work together; we do not have to agree with each other, but we do need to generously respect one another's views.

The case I am trying to make is that any chaplaincy team must be multifaith so that it can competently support people of different faiths and act with integrity as faith advisers to the companies for their particular faith.

4

The Role of Wisdom
Alongside Ethics,
Values and Culture

Wisdom in faith traditions

As a multifaith chaplaincy team we are committed to offer assistance in promoting the role and value of wisdom from a faith perspective, as it helps to bring a more integrated approach and give a wider context to values and ethics. In the long term, helping employees to take joint responsibility for decisions and actions benefits the company, its core business and the wider community.

A well-tried and tested method for sharing wisdom from different faith traditions is to use Scriptural Reasoning, which has been developed over many years by Professor David Ford with the Cambridge Interfaith Programme (CIP). Scriptural Reasoning began with Jews, Muslims and Christians coming together to discuss and study each other's religious texts. It now provides a practical and helpful framework and is practised in many settings, universities, schools, churches, synagogues and mosques as well as secular institutions such as prisons and business communities. The process is perhaps best described on the website of the CIP:[14]

In Scriptural Reasoning (SR), participants meet to read passages from their respective sacred texts. Together they discuss the content of those texts, and the variety of ways in which their traditions have worked with them and continue to work with them, and the ways in which those texts shape their understanding of and engagement with a range of contemporary issues. The goal is not agreement but rather growth in understanding one another's traditions and deeper exploration of the texts and their possible interpretations.

As a chaplaincy we offered the opportunity to a group of businessmen and women from the Abrahamic faiths in Canary Wharf to share wisdom from their own scriptural texts and explore how this might positively influence their workplaces. We invited Professor David Ford and a team from the CIP to facilitate a session with the chosen topic 'Leadership and Communication', as it was business focused. Afterwards, we asked people to feed back on their experience of how they had found the event, and they said things like: 'Exposure to other faiths, which I don't normally have even though I work daily with both Jews and Muslims' and 'Interesting being with people of other faiths in such a context and working on understanding text together'. We also asked if they would recommend Scriptural Reasoning to their company or colleagues, and we had very positive comments, such as: 'Yes, an opportunity to reflect and learn from others' and 'Yes, could be an interesting team-building exercise to encourage communications etc.'

My observation of using the process of Scriptural Reasoning with business people of faith was that it was a non-threatening exercise. It generated a very stimulating and thought-provoking conversation around issues faced in the workplace, leading to a deeper respect for each other's faiths and the wisdom they can bring to the workplace. When we study the scriptures together it is amazing how often something that might seem irrelevant can actually cause us to think afresh and challenge our contemporary ideas and thoughts, reminding us about justice, social inclusion, equality, behaviour and so on as we share our reflections together.

Acknowledging that each of us, whatever our background, can contribute wisdom to the workplace is important for instilling trust and integrity. Another important theme linked to wisdom is our search for meaning and purpose in all that we do, often referred to as vocation. This chapter will explore wisdom and vocation from a faith perspective and the added value they can bring to the workplace in assisting with the current challenges facing many organizations within the private, public and voluntary sectors and enabling these organizations to embed a good ethical and values culture of working practices.

The global financial crisis opened doors for discussion around religion

When I was reading through the World Economic Forum website not long after the beginning of the global financial crisis, I came across the quote commonly attributed to Adam Smith (1723–1790).

> Markets could not flourish without a strong underlying moral culture, animated by empathy and fellow-feeling, by our ability to understand our common bond as human beings and to recognize the needs of others.

Adam Smith was the Scottish social philosopher and political economist, whose substantive works are collected within the book *The Wealth of Nations*. His ideas were a reflection on economics in light of the beginning of the Industrial Revolution, and he stated that free-market economies (i.e., capitalist ones) were the most productive and beneficial to societies. He argued for an economic system based on an underlying strong moral culture, on government, and social and individual morality as they affect the operations of the market economy. I wonder what he would have thought about the factors that led to the credit crunch.

As we are all too well aware, what began with the initial credit crunch led to a global financial crisis, where governments had to bail out banks and a number of countries needed drastic financial measures to prevent their economies from collapsing. The financial institution lost public trust and faced much criticism from many directions. Since this time, the behaviour and culture of the banks and bankers have been under intense scrutiny, and questions have been asked such as: how did this happen? How can we ensure that this never happens again? Governments, the World Bank, the Bank of England, the Federal Reserve, the EU Bank and so on believed that a contributing factor to the crisis was inadequate regulation of the financial industry and the banks' activities. Consequently, various financial regulators around the world underwent internal structural changes to improve their power and oversight to impose sanctions on banks' misbehaviour. The Financial Services Authority in the UK was split into two organizations: the Financial Conduct Authority and the Prudential Regulatory Authority.

Throughout this time there has been much debate as to the effectiveness of imposed regulation compared with self-regulation, and the need to change the banking culture. A senior banker commented to me that both kinds of regulation are needed; bankers are bright people and if regulation is limited to compliance and keeping rules then a way around them will always be found. Often the debates around self-regulation are about how an institution regulates itself, but institutions embody a community of individuals, therefore compliance and self-regulation must be the responsibility of both the institution and the employees within it. Self-regulation is needed; individual bankers need to understand that they are members of the banking community and therefore responsible and accountable for their own moral and ethical behaviour in taking wise decisions and actions.

As chaplains, we understand from our experience as members of faith communities that human beings are relational and flourish more fully in a community than in isolation, and from within a community where wisdom is shared and behaviour can be learnt. Global banks are much more than a system or faceless structure; within them is a diverse community of people working together to deliver all the core activities. So when senior business leaders talk of changing the banking culture within their organizations, they are recreating an internal culture to ensure that their employees participate as responsible members of the community, living out their espoused values and ethical standards in the way they deliver all their bank's core activities.

While many of my comments are influenced by my own business context and the particular issues I have witnessed, I think it is always useful to reflect on the culture and practices of any organization or business that we might be involved with. For example, employees need to gain an understanding that they are part of a wider working community. For many working within their industry, it may not be easy to instantly recognize the way their particular role or job contributes when they seem a long way down the chain from the final product the general public sees or experiences. Nevertheless, it is important to help employees to see that what they do, and fundamentally how they do it, matters to the larger purposes of the organization. The story is told of how the former US President John F. Kennedy once visited the NASA headquarters. He came across a cleaner and asked him what his job was. The cleaner replied, 'My job is to help to put a man on the moon.' There is some discussion of whether this story is true or not, but what it illustrates is the cleaner's understanding that his role within the community of NASA was part of the whole process of putting a man on the moon.

Businesses are aware that for espoused values and ethics to take root, it must be a communal activity and their employees' importance for the business and the wider community must be made clear. Each employee has a part to play. Often when referring to an individual's values and ethics, the term 'moral compass' is used, which the Cambridge Dictionary defines as a natural feeling that makes people know what is right and wrong and how they should behave. As a chaplain, I want to suggest that it is more than a 'feeling' that is natural but is rooted in something deeper, a conscience that is shaped by background, upbringing, education, nationality and, for some, religious belief. The values and ethics expected of us within the workplace should not be seen in isolation from the rest of a person's life but should provide the magnetic 'pull' of their 'moral compass' and be intrinsically linked with how they live within a community – in this context the local workplace community – and its relationship with the global community. A report by the World Economic Forum (2014) underlines how faith contributes to this, stating, 'Faith permeates our world, providing a moral and ethical compass for the vast majority of people.' When we ask people to put their faith in a separate box and leave it outside, then the company they work for and they themselves are poorer for it. Stephen Green, formerly Group Chairman of HSBC, comments further when he says, 'Compartmentalization is a refuge from ambiguity; it enables us to simplify the rules by which we live in our different realms of life, and avoid, if we are not careful, the moral and spiritual questions' (Green 2009, p.18).

To implement any cultural change within an organization, it is important that employees are integrated so that their behaviour is consistent at work and at home, and any good change in behaviour is long lasting. There also needs to be a clear understanding that 'wilful' bad behaviour will not be tolerated. Key to building a good working culture is the creation of an environment where shared values (including moral and spiritual) and ethics are core to all working practices and responsibility is given to employees to determine what is the right thing to do and act on. I grew up in a generation that learnt the mantra, 'If you want a job done properly, then do it yourself.' However, this is unhelpful, and if we want people to learn to take responsibility, then we have to trust them and give them the opportunities to do so. Engaging the whole team is important, because it draws on the diversity of their experience, culture and knowledge. The process involved may not be simple but complex and require more than just following a set of rules; it will need experience, wisdom and careful consideration of all the information available at the time.

Moral and spiritual questions are important and can assist with the consideration for the wider and maybe long-term implications of an action or decision. They also can be helpful for dealing with genuine human mistakes or misjudgements, encouraging a positive atmosphere for people to own up or seek help to sort out issues and move forward before things become catastrophic. It is important that asking moral and spiritual questions is seen as strength and not weakness and that it is understood that they contribute to the collective wisdom within any team.

Within any organization, the issue about how the behaviour of senior managers and boards is held to account is crucial, not just in their regulatory compliance (and many industries are regulated), but also in the eyes of the general public. The most recent public example of this is the UK government and regulators introducing the new Senior Managers Regime for the banks, which came into effect in March 2016. This clarifies the lines of responsibility at the top of banks and enhances the regulators' ability to hold senior individuals in banks to account and require banks to regularly vet their senior managers for fitness and propriety.

However, while it is important and necessary to hold senior managers accountable in any business, whether in the private, public or voluntary sectors, it is crucial that all managers at every level and all employees understand that they too need to learn to take responsibility for their decisions and actions and the consequences that might result. For example, I was having coffee with a senior executive who had been involved in a redundancy process for his department. He looked exhausted and told me how wretched and uncomfortable it made him feel. He said it was important for him to face the people he was letting go in his department and not hide behind human resources personnel. People tell me they are overwhelmed with the number of emails they receive each day, and struggle to give them the same attention and deliberation as a face-to-face conversation, but that they are aware of the importance of each decision.

When work appears relentless or we feel undervalued, how do we keep motivated?

Vocation plays an important role in people's self-understanding in terms of the job they do and how they do it. This was brought home to me in an encounter with a female human resources director with an EMEA role in the field of diversity and inclusion, and employee engagement. She was in the process of leaving her current job and moving to another global bank to take on a more senior global role. We were having breakfast together and talking about her new role. She said, 'I now understand my vocation and ministry. One of the things I have learnt by working with you is that my ministry is to create a good working environment for people. I believe that's been my ministry in my present job, and I believe that will be my ministry in my new job.'

As we talked I was very excited; this person had got it! I guess it has been my hobby horse that Christians should understand their vocation within the workplace. So often we think about vocation, or even ask someone if they have a vocation; from a Christian perspective we usually mean to be a priest or maybe become a member of a religious community. Sometimes it is used to include healthcare workers or teachers. The radical shift that the Reformation brought in terms of the idea of vocation is often forgotten by church leaders. The word vocation comes from the Latin word '*vocare*' meaning to call – a vocation is God's calling to a particular set of activities in life and to live them out as well as we are able. Martin Luther understood this and taught that all life was to be lived in response to a generous God. Both Martin Luther and John Calvin believed firmly that every Christian's response to this generous God was to serve God in the world. This was the first time that everyday activities were given religious significance and thus had implications for economic life. Calvin's thinking changed the Christian view on 'usury'; he based his approval of taking interest in accordance with the economic shift he observed in his time. He did not approve of professional bankers, only of loans between individuals for commercial ventures. However, Daniel Finn (2013) suggests that Calvin has not yet carried his argument to its logical conclusion that, if done responsibly, the occupation of the banker can be morally respectable.

The reformers no longer saw a separation between the sacred and the secular – all activities that serve God and God's creation were of value – and this shows, even 400 years ago, the value and contribution that faith could have on everyday life, including economic life and the workplace. I realize that the words sacred and secular are not normally used by most people in everyday conversation, but I think they do have an influence on our lives. We do not consciously divide our world into sacred and secular, but this dichotomy is a result of centuries of religious thinking and teachings. The National Secular Society readily talks about a 'secular' world by which it means one 'without God or anything religious'. Many of us might think of the sacred in terms of going into a religious building or attending a religious act of worship; however, I believe it is more than this. I wonder how many of us send up that quick prayer when nothing else seems to work, or when perhaps we have observed an amazing sunset and think 'wow' or been enthralled by a piece of music that has moved us; there is something about these things that is not easily defined by a rational explanation. It is bringing all this together – the rational and that which is hard to define in our emotions and feelings – that drives or motivates us in how we think and act. We bring together every part of us, often referred to as body, mind and spirit, into every context we find ourselves either at work or at home, in the gym and of course our place of worship if we practise a faith.

When we think about vocation we think about what it is that motivates us to do what we do. Although the language of vocation has its roots in Christianity, Christians don't have the monopoly on its use. While Muslims and Jews as well as other faiths may not use the terminology, I am sure they would agree that they too are called to serve God in whatever activities they undertake in the world, whether at work or at home.

The sense of having vocation within the workplace is helpful for all employees not just people of faith, as it is important to understand what motivates and inspires us to do a task and do it well. This idea is one that might resonate with the Millennials in the workplace who find it easier to do a task with enthusiasm if they understand the meaning and purpose behind it. What's the point? Who does it benefit? Why are we doing this? While having sense of vocation may not answer all their immediate questions, it does provide that bigger picture of which we are a small part. I illustrated this earlier when I mentioned the cleaner at NASA. He was part of a team and he understood that his particular job, however small, had a role to play in the overall task of getting a man on the moon. The understanding that we all have a vocation needs to be worked out in our daily lives – what it means for today, where we are and in whatever we are doing – remembering that the underlying concept of vocation is a calling to serve others in the world. This in turn brings with it a responsibility to care for the creation, to help the poor and needy, to bring about the kind of justice which directs all our actions towards the common good for all of humanity.

The twentieth-century writer and Christian theologian Dorothy L. Sayers described vocation:

> Work is not primarily a thing one does to live but the thing one lives to do. It is, or it should be, the full expression of the worker's faculties, the thing in which he [or she] finds spiritual, mental and bodily satisfaction, and the medium in which he [or she] offers himself [or herself] to God.
>
> (Sayers 1946, p.122)

Many of us spend a large part of our lives in the workplace, and with an ever-increasing life expectancy, the amount of time for each generation will only increase as the pension age continues to rise. So if we are to have good values and ethics contributing to a good work culture, then it is helpful for people to have a sense of vocation within their working lives.

While a sense of vocation is helpful it is not enough in itself; it needs to be worked out in the way we contribute to the working environment and the core business of the company we work for.

The importance of wisdom for commerce and community

> An intelligent mind acquires knowledge, the ear of the wise seeks knowledge.
>
> (Proverbs 18.15)

> Listen to advice and accept instruction, that you may gain wisdom for the future.
>
> (Proverbs 19.20)

> Ben Zoma used to say: 'Who is wise? The one who learns from every man, for it is written (Psalms 119.99) "From all my teachers I gained understanding, for Your testimonies are my conversation."'
>
> (Mishnah Ethics of our Fathers 4:1)

He (God) gives wisdom to whom He wills, and one
to whom wisdom is given, they have truly been given
abundant good. But none remember except people
of understanding.

(Qur'an 2:269)

If we want employees to take responsibility for their
decisions and actions in instigating behavioural change and
consequently changing the culture of an organization, then we
need to acknowledge what they can contribute to this process.
Therefore I will explore in this section why the role of wisdom
could be important in contributing to the positive role and the
influence faith can have within the workplace.

As my understanding of our specific chaplaincy context
changed with my awareness of the challenges and issues
which face this specific working community, the emphasis of
the chaplaincy began to change. The global financial crisis
prompted me to ask questions such as: what is the role of
the chaplaincy now? What should the chaplaincy be doing?
The answer to these questions in the first instance, as I have
mentioned earlier, was to listen to the stories of the business
community. Another strong influence was a comment made
by Jim Wallis, the public theologian and international
commentator on ethics and public life. At the World Economic
Forum in January 2009, he said that the wrong question was
being asked of the world's political and business leaders. It
should not be 'When will the crisis be over?' but 'How will
this crisis change us?' (Wallis 2010, p.3). This has inspired
me and shaped my thinking about the role of faith within
the workplace.

When I refer to wisdom, I mean more than expertise.
Wisdom is formed in the ongoing life of a particular community
– and this includes the business community – where it is lived
out and exercised. Wisdom is more than a set of rules to be
followed; it is about using all the knowledge and experience
at our disposal to inform our choices and actions. It recognizes

that people of faith or indeed no faith have something to add to the discussion/debate/decision within any conversation of any group of people. It respects and listens attentively to people who have different perspectives and hold different views. Wisdom works itself out in the real world, and it is a communal process.

Wisdom can provide a space for overlap between faith and the workplace practices for achieving the core business of the company. As part of a multifaith chaplaincy, my colleagues and I are able to help in this space and assist people of faith to draw on their own religious tradition of wisdom. Christian wisdom literature has its origins in Jewish wisdom literature. Islam too has a tradition of wisdom literature. However, wisdom is not confined just to the Abrahamic faiths, it is also part of the tradition of Greek and other Western philosophies, Buddhism, Hinduism, Chinese and Japanese religious philosophies as well as secular humanism. These traditions too bring a wealth of wisdom.

Speaking from my own Christian tradition, I find the definition of Christian wisdom, by the theologian Miroslav Volf (2011, p.101) helpful. He says that the Christian faith provides 'an overarching interpretation of reality, a set of convictions, attitudes and practices that direct people to living their lives well'. Wisdom, therefore, encourages an integrated way of life that enables the flourishing of individuals, communities and all creation.

When I think about wisdom and reflect on the values that companies and most organizations are embracing, such as integrity, honesty, fairness, respect, responsibility, openness, transparency, trust and courage, there are clear similarities within religion. Faiths have a long tradition of pursuing wisdom, developing ethical thinking and promoting values for good behaviour. The Institute of Business Ethics (Webley 2014) has highlighted in a recent report the key themes that repeat themselves in the scriptures of the Christian,

Jewish and Muslim faiths and form the basis of any human relationship that is lived out within a community. They are: justice (fairness), mutual respect (love and consideration), stewardship (trusteeship) and honesty (truthfulness). All the world faiths share some equivalent of the Golden Rule, or 'do unto others as you would want them to do to you' (see the Appendix for a summary of the Golden Rule from different faith traditions). Some in the business world would say this in itself is not enough to ensure that all employees understand what is expected of them in their working relationships when faced with an ethical dilemma. Therefore, they suggest a slightly modified version of the Rule: 'Treat others as you want to be treated.'

While the use of the word wisdom may not be part of everyday office language, David Ford (2014, p.25) reflects that, 'Even when the word "wisdom" is not used, it is often present through concerns for sound, intelligent judgement and decision making, prudent discernment of priorities, long term flourishing of people and societies...combining knowledge, values and appropriate practices.' While I am discussing wisdom from a faith perspective, it is important to recognize that people who would say that they have no faith allegiance still have much wisdom to contribute to decisions and actions. It is important to note that wisdom is not a static activity but evolves and changes as our understanding or situation changes.

As a result of my own reflections on the role of wisdom, I began to explore its place, particularly from a faith perspective, as an addition to the prophetic voice of judgement expressed by faith communities and the churches. In listening to the business community I explored the place for the voice of wisdom in response to the following questions: what have we learnt, how do we move forward, what will we do differently, and who can help us? These guiding questions changed the nature of conversations and discussions I had with people. The individuals became less defensive and more willing to talk about what had gone wrong, why it had gone wrong and what needed to be addressed. This approach gave people a voice, in all parts of the organization, from a chief executive officer who was willing to talk about what had happened in the banking crisis, to a conversation with a personal assistant who was having difficult conversations with her family around the banking crisis as they did not want to listen to her viewpoint. So for me, listening and trying to understand was key, and even if what was said was difficult to fathom, it was still the beginning of wisdom.

Wisdom is worked out within a community. It is desirable that each individual employee understands that his or her job is an essential part of the bank's core activities provided by the whole bank community. Hence responsibility becomes shared and not just an individual's endeavour. Humans are relational beings and work more effectively when there is shared wisdom, mutual respect and trust within a group or team. When we begin to explore the use of wisdom it goes beyond a box-ticking exercise, or asking ourselves whether we have followed the right practice or procedure, or checked the ethics and values manual. The values become lived out within the working community, the ethics are discussed, people's contributions are taken into account and a decision becomes shared. I remember having a conversation with a faculty manager when I was a university chaplain, who confided that her department was going through a period of change and her team was becoming very difficult to manage. As the conversation progressed she mentioned that she had been too busy to have the usual weekly team meetings, and I gently suggested that this very basic oversight might be part of the problem. A few weeks later we met again and she mentioned that she had reinstated the weekly team meetings and the team now felt more involved in the process. She added that this had transformed her working relationship with her team.

Within Christianity, a key feature of wisdom is humility. Put simply, it means that we have a responsibility as part of the community to admit when we need help, we don't know or we have made a mistake, and to say sorry. We need to recognize it is our duty to do this as soon as we realize there is an issue rather than getting deeper into a mess that could have catastrophic consequences. There is an important flip side, which is forgiveness, and it is essential to have a mechanism or strategy for dealing with genuine mistakes or misjudgement and the willingness to learn from the situation and restore trust.

Some of the characteristics of a wise manager might be as follows: one who tries to combine knowledge, experience, self-awareness, understanding, good judgement and far-sighted decision making with good team management skills, justice, fairness, honesty and humility, setting a good example and an expectation that his or her team or department will follow this, not just as individuals but together.

So far I have discussed the importance of wisdom and how faith can play an important part in promoting an integrated approach to give a wider context to values and ethics. At the beginning of this chapter I mentioned the effectiveness of the sharing of wisdom using the process of Scriptural Reasoning and how we have used it in Canary Wharf. I now want to give a home-grown example of how the members of the Abrahamic faiths within the business community developed the Common Faith Covenant for doing good business.

The Common Faith Covenant

One of the important features of being a chaplain is to understand and know your context and work with people in it. It was precisely this that enabled me to develop the Common Faith Covenant, because it grew out of listening and working with members of the Canary Wharf business community. I believe it could have much wider influence than just the financial sector.

I began a process in 2010 as a response to the financial crisis that began in 2008. Although there were a number of initiatives responding to the financial crisis, including a series of annual conferences on the theme 'Trust and Values in the City' hosted by various Lord Mayors of London, as chaplain in Canary Wharf I wanted to offer something locally for this community. To help determine what might be useful, I attended a number of external interfaith events such as lectures, seminars and conferences to explore the issues that led to the failures of the financial industry. Many of the events were addressed by economists, academics, theologians and faith groups, or senior leaders from particular faith communities. However, none of the events appeared to include much positive dialogue with those working within the financial sector to help them move forward in their various roles from this crisis.

It seemed to me that we had reached a Kairos moment within the financial industry. The previous couple of years we had seen the banks as very defensive, with criticism and pressure coming at them from all sides. I wanted as a chaplaincy to do something different to fulfil the following criteria:

- It needed to be specifically aimed at the financial organizations and businesses based in Canary Wharf.

- It needed to include and engage bankers in the discussions around the issues moving forward, rather than speak about them and their failures.

- It needed to be transformative.

I embarked on a series of discussions with a number of senior people from different faiths who worked in financial and professional services, to gauge their views on what might be the most appropriate way forward. It was not intended that any event would be about the bankers justifying themselves, but I believed that those working within the financial sector were now ready and would welcome an opportunity to engage in a process in which they could not only be honest in owning the failure of the financial system, but more importantly explore ways to move forward to recover the trust of the governments and ordinary people as well as continue to contribute to the local, national and international economies.

The suggestion came from a senior Muslim banker that he would host a round-table discussion over dinner if the chaplaincy would organize it. I invited senior business men and women from the financial and professional services, who belonged to one of the Abrahamic faiths, as a starting point to explore 'Faith and Integrity in the Workplace'. The discussion was facilitated by Philippa Foster Back, Director of the Institute of Business Ethics, and took place in November 2011. Our discussion focused around three questions:

- What kinds of day-to-day ethical issues or dilemmas are we facing in our teams today?

- How can we change the culture in our organizations?

- How do you take your values home, back into society?

At the end of the dinner, it was agreed that the group would meet again with the same facilitator. In fact, the group meet three times over the next couple of years, with various people joining at different times.

During the final round-table discussion, the group were clear that they wished for something tangible to reflect their commitment and resolution to move things forward and their personal commitment to do so. By this time many of the banks were in the process of working hard to change their internal culture and to encourage their employees to engage in good working practices. The group wanted to give the message to people of faith that their personal and professional values were integrated and to provide a collective strength for their own behaviour within this stressful environment.

They agreed that it would be helpful to provide an opportunity for people of faith to articulate publicly that, through their faith values, they contribute to good and ethical business practices in the workplace. From this series of conversations with these business leaders we created together a positive faith framework for doing business, which we called the Common Faith Covenant. The framework of this covenant is as follows:

- Live by the principles of openness, fairness, mutual respect and stewardship.[15]

- Treat other people as you would want them to treat you.

- If necessary, have courage to speak up.

- Be accountable to God in all you do.

We hope that by providing this we are able to give people of faith an opportunity to make a statement that faith is an important part of their lives and it impacts on how they contribute to the core business of the companies they work for.

Although this covenant originated through conversations with members of the Jewish, Christian and Muslim faiths who all share origins in the biblical figure Abraham, the intention is that it is not limited to just these world faiths. It is our hope that all people of faith will feel able to adopt this in their working lives and be part of a visible community that shows that faith can make a positive contribution to public life.

We used the phrase Common Faith Covenant rather than something like Common Ethical Values as we wanted to convey something deeper than just signing up to a set of values. The concept of a covenant is found within faith, particularly the Abrahamic faiths. A covenant is understood as a promise, which in its basic sense is a binding, enduring relationship of mutual loyalty between people. A covenant focuses on the relationship between those who have entered into it rather than just on the stipulated obligations and enduring responsibilities, although these of course are an important outworking of it. Within the Jewish tradition, the former Chief Rabbi Lord Jonathan Sacks writes:

> A covenant is about loyalty…a covenant is about identity, about belonging to something bigger than me. From a covenant, I am transformed. I am no longer the person I once was, but am part of something larger than I once was. Thus, a social contract creates a State, but a covenant creates society.
>
> (Sacks 2011)

Within the Muslim tradition, a covenant, similar to Christianity and Judaism, has its foundations in how the people of faith relate to God. 'It is used and understood to be universal and pre-temporal before the beginning of creation (Qur'an 7:172). It is also understood as a promise – a promise made by God and a promise made by the human being (Qur'an 2:40). The Qur'an draws attention to the reciprocal dimension of the covenant. God elevates and honours the human being by taking a covenant from them. The human being honours God by obeying Him and fulfilling His commands.'[16] Therefore, we used the word covenant to signify something more than just a commitment to keep a set of values, but a promise bound up in something which unites the faith communities in the way their faith informs and underpins their behaviour and actions for doing good business.

Interestingly, the Canary Wharf Multifaith Chaplaincy is not the only organization offering a personal ethical framework for the business community. In 2016 I was at a conference and discovered that the Dutch government in an attempt to restore public trust in the banking industry has introduced a Bankers' Oath, which, since April 2015, all bankers from the senior managers down are expected to take. Interestingly, it has a religious element, as part of the oath is as follows: 'I swear that I will endeavor to maintain and promote confidence in the financial sector. So help me God' (*The New York Times* 2016).

It should be noted that professional oaths are not new; indeed the medical profession has had the Hippocratic Oath since about the fifth century BCE. It is one of the oldest binding documents in history, and the Oath written by Hippocrates is still held sacred by physicians.

As I explored further I discovered another example from The Ethics Centre, based in Sydney, Australia. It is an industry-led initiative which established the Banking and Finance Oath in 2012 (BFO 2012) to restore trust and encourage ethical behaviour in the financial services industry. The oath contains a set of commitments that individuals working in the banking and finance industry adopt and apply as personal principles in their work. In summoning up the oath they say, 'In these and all other matters; My word is my bond.' This is an interesting use of 'my word is my bond', which had for centuries been the motto of the London Stock Exchange and until computerization transformed investment banking and allowed deregulation of the Stock Exchange, this was deemed enough to instil trust in transactions and between parties.

Over the years since the global financial crisis, the global economy and the banking industry in particular have continued to be under the spotlight. Much has been achieved in the global banks in terms of ethics training and reforming banking culture both internally and externally. However, the banking environment continues to be stressful, given continued changes in financial regulation across the world, the current uncertainties in the global economy and the pressures on a bank to make a profit for its customers and shareholders.

The practical implications of these seem to be a process of ongoing internal restructuring, or relocation of employees out of Canary Wharf or relocating roles that were previously done in London to other parts of the world. All this leads to uncertainty and anxiety. At times like this it is helpful to remind people of faith that their personal and professional values when integrated give a collective strength for their own behaviour and provide opportunities to articulate publicly that they, through their faith values, contribute to good and ethical business practices in the workplace.

Conclusion

In this chapter I have discussed how the global financial crisis has triggered an implementation of change of culture within the banking sector in terms of embedding the core values and ethics of a bank. Within this I have outlined the importance of all employees, not just managers, taking responsibility for their decisions and actions in changing the behaviour of that organization. I have then suggested that a sense of vocation is helpful in giving an understanding of purpose and meaning to people's work and therefore assists in motivating the entire workforce.

Underlying this has been a discussion about the role of wisdom in the workplace and how the different faiths which have long wisdom traditions can contribute to helping individuals and teams take responsibility, as they bring all the wisdom within that team to bear when discussing the right decision or course of action that might be needed.

Team leadership is crucial. Recently, I was introduced to the phrase, 'the shadow of the leader'. It refers to the fact that whether the leader and his or her team understand it or not, their collective and individual behaviour casts a positive or negative shadow across the entire organization. Actions speak louder than words, and it is important therefore that there is a consistency between what is expected and what actually happens in reality. It made me reflect that my faith and actions as a Christian leader will cast a shadow, in the same way as the actions and beliefs of other leaders do in their own contexts. There is a consequence in all we do, even if we try to convince ourselves that no one is watching!

5

Understanding Mission in the Context of Chaplaincy

What is mission?

In the previous chapter I have written generally about how the Canary Wharf Multifaith Chaplaincy was established and how it built relationships with the companies and individuals and the importance of becoming a multifaith chaplaincy. It is my intention that this book will attract an audience from both the business community and from faith leaders and adherents. Therefore, from time to time my discussions of various themes might seem more relevant for faith leaders and their communities. However, given the increasing role of faith within the public arena, it might be helpful for business leaders to understand these themes and hence assist in overcoming some of the anxieties about faith in the workplace, and indeed see that not all conversations around faith are unhelpful.

I was listening to the Sunday Programme on Radio 4 on the last day of the Rio Olympics in 2016. They were having a conversation about whether it was appropriate to mention one's faith in the world of sport. As I listened, it became clear to me that in many parts of the world for the competing athletes it was natural to mention God or even thank God for the results achieved. It is only the northern European countries that seem unhappy with this. The diversity of athletes taking part at the

Olympics and the importance of their faith is mirrored in the business world.

In this chapter, I want to explore the concept of mission. While we are all familiar with this word within the business world, it is helpful to understand that it also has a religious significance. This is especially important to grasp because, unlike most of the other world religions, Christianity and Islam are interested in attracting and converting non-believers and people of other traditions. So within chaplaincy it is important to acknowledge this and reflect on how this plays out within the chaplaincy team in our relationships and working practices, and how this influences the kind of activities that the informal faith groups within the companies might be seeking to arrange. As I am a Christian chaplain, and in the UK and the USA the largest faith group is Christian both in the workplace and in society in general, much of this discourse will be from a Christian perspective, but I hope the themes and models explored are transferable and offer some guidance as to how other faiths interact too.

As chaplains we minister in the complex secular environment of Canary Wharf, with its international, multicultural and highly diverse working community where people have a variety of lifestyles, cultures and beliefs. So from the outset in writing this chapter I want to be clear that I completely understand the sensitivities of the context and our activities appreciate this. We are aware that as chaplains we are welcome guests on the private business estate and within the offices of the global companies, and our behaviour must be in accordance with this.

In many conversations I have had with Christian chaplains from other sectors, especially healthcare chaplains, they mostly shy away from the word 'mission' as it often focuses on the word 'proselytize' and all the baggage that implies. Indeed, Canary Wharf Group and the global companies made it clear to me that chaplains who proselytize are not welcome.

However, this should not mean that chaplains can't mention their faith, or are unable to engage in mission. Often the words evangelism and mission are used interchangeably, but actually they are not synonymous.

However, to put the readers' minds at rest, I work with a much wider definition of mission. From a Christian chaplain's viewpoint, my definition is 'helping Christians to live their daily lives as integrated people, whose faith has an impact on their behaviour and relationships within their workplaces, and when asked using the opportunity to reflect on things from a Christian perspective'. For me it is about having clarity that as a person of faith this should influence our behaviour, and yes we can talk about our faith but only when asked rather than seeking every opportunity to button hole people. I remember when I worked in industry as a research scientist, there were Christians in my research group who regularly tried to strike up an evangelistic conversation with people at the drinks machine! The result was that members of the team would only go to the machine in a small group (safety in numbers); these conversations were unwelcome and inappropriate. I had a recent conversation with my Muslim colleague and asked his opinion, given that both Christianity and Islam are interested in attracting converts. He affirmed his would be a similar position as the Muslim chaplain to me as the Christian one, and he said that it is important to be respectful of one's context, but that Muslims are expected to honour God in the workplace and talk about their faith, but only when appropriate.

The gift of hospitality

For their own wellbeing, people should be able to bring their whole selves into the workplace and that includes their faith, which means that from time to time conversations around faith will arise. For meaningful and respectful conversations to take place within the workplace that share ideas and practices from different faiths, it seems to me that being generously hospitable plays an important part.

Hospitality is a central principle of many of the world religions and cultures; it is extended not just as a courtesy but as an obligation. The Hindu scriptures prescribe that the householder should treat the unexpected guest as God and no matter how poor one might be, should offer three things: sweet words, a sitting place and refreshment (even if it is only a glass of water). Sikh hospitality is well known in the offering of food freely to guests. For Buddhists, hospitality is assumed within the teaching of Dana. This is shown not so much in the act of giving but there has to be a feeling of wanting to give, which expresses itself in the kindness in welcoming guests or strangers.

A powerful hospitality motif shared within Christianity, Islam and Judaism is seen in the figure of Abraham. He responds as host to three visitors, feeding them and giving them shelter, unaware that he is in fact entertaining angels. 'By this act, Abraham inspired a theology of hospitality often echoed in Jewish, Christian and Islamic literature and used as a framework for interreligious dialogue' (Siddiqui 2015, p.10).

In the narrative that precedes this event we discover that Abraham has set out from his hometown, following a promise that God had made to him to bring him to a new land and to make him the father of a great nation that would be a blessing to all nations. From his journeying, Abraham had experienced being a stranger in a foreign land where he was dependant on the hospitality of others. So it was his immediate response when visited by the three strangers to offer them generous hospitality. Both with the Christian and the Jewish tradition, the offering of hospitality to strangers is a strong theme. Within Islam, the virtue of hospitality lies at the very basis of the Islamic ethical system, which has its roots in the pre-Islamic Bedouin culture of welcome and generosity in the harsh desert environment.

> Indeed, hosting the guest or welcoming the stranger is a central event in the world's great wisdom traditions. Many state that the stranger embodies the presence of God and brings blessings in multiple ways. Furthermore, ideas of reciprocity, unconditionally in the act of hospitality, are central to current religious and ethical thinking.
>
> (Siddiqui 2015, p.11)

It is easy to offer hospitality to family or friends or people who are like-minded. The concept of offering hospitality to the stranger or traveller is the basic quality of compassion and challenges us in our generosity not only in material terms but in emotional and psychological terms. It demands a generosity where the role of host and guest are interchangeable by each party. Hospitality should be offered willingly. Within the workplace, hospitality works itself out in relationships where there is a mutual willingness to listen and appreciate the wisdom and ideas of each other, as we share from our different cultures or backgrounds, and to exhibit a generosity even if we disagree.

Conversations around faith can be helpful

The boundaries and parameters in which chaplains operate are less formal than those required for professional counsellors, but no less professional. Often chaplains will operate in a very relaxed environment; in Canary Wharf we meet with people in the informality of a coffee shop. It is important that in any conversation that a chaplain takes part in, they recognize that they do so in the knowledge that they will be respectful of the faith tradition of the person they are chatting with, or if they have no faith, that will be respected too. It goes without saying that any one-to-one conversation with chaplains will be confidential and non-judgemental. Having said that, we often discover that people want to talk about God and we find that it is often not the concept of God that people have trouble with, but institutionalized religions.

We live in a fast-paced globalized world, with instant communications, relationships worked out on social media, and often long distances lived way from family. Many people do not have the luxury of sitting around the kitchen table at the end of the day with family or friends to chat about how things are going. We find as chaplains that often this is the role that many people are looking for, an opportunity for a face-to-face conversation with someone who has time to listen and help them reflect on a particular situation or decision. Interestingly, in a recent conversation with a group of Millennials who are very social media savvy, I discovered that they still prefer to meet face to face and use social media just to facilitate meeting up. We find when we meet with people, sometimes, just listening and reflecting the conversation back is enough. At other times, people want to explore questions of faith and how it might help them.

Often exploratory conversations within a non-threatening environment can contribute to a person's self-understanding, and can help them in their exploration of the questions around the meaning and purpose of life in general. Even if the person is of no faith it is hoped that the conversations have added to the pool of wisdom in helping them with the decision or action they are about to make.

With all the continued challenges people face within the workplace, we offer the opportunity to talk about how the traditions of their own faith contribute to their values and ethics, how their faith can helpfully influence behaviour and decision making in their workplace, and their relationships with colleagues and clients.

A Christian perspective on mission

Traditionally, chaplaincy has been Christian in the UK, with teams generally comprising an Anglican chaplain, a Roman

Catholic chaplain and a Free Church chaplain (usually a Baptist, Methodist or United Reformed Church minister). Although the first chaplains recorded were Anglican priests, deployed by King Henry VIII on his warships, more recently, chaplaincy teams in sectors such as health, education, military and prisons have added chaplains of other faiths, reflecting the changing nature of our society.

Although I am writing from a Church of England perspective, I am aware that other Christian traditions will have their own particular approach to mission. The Church of England probably provided the first chaplains within most sectors and has had, I think, an influence on the development of the services and working practices of all chaplains, both Christian and other faiths. In all conversations around faith, whether more formal such as the process of Scriptural Reasoning mentioned in the previous chapter or informal over a coffee, it is important to ensure that the conversation happens in way that is mutually respectful and non-coercive.

In an earlier chapter I outlined some key features of the Church of England, which as the established church has particular obligations and responsibilities that other Christian denominations do not have. These have helped to shape the work of chaplaincy and its mission. Within this section I chart my own exploration and thinking and those that have influenced me as a Christian chaplain in building non-coercive working models of chaplaincy in the different contexts that I have worked in.

Of major importance for me has been understanding the role and nature of the Church of England – that it is not a membership organization, nor is it congregationally based. But it is parish based and its mission is to be inclusive and welcoming and hold together different traditions within it: evangelical, liberal Catholic, Anglo Catholic and everything in between.

The Church of England and other Christian denominations have been shaped by the Reformation, when the Bible became accessible in the vernacular, together with church services. In Anglicanism truth is revealed through scripture within the Christian tradition (though this is not exclusively represented by the authority of the Church as an institution), and human reason is a valued component. Theological enquiry is welcomed not just from academics but from all Christians as we are all encouraged to enquire after truth. This balance of scripture, reason and tradition is the hallmark of the Church of England and has been influential in shaping me as a person and as a chaplain. Scripture, reason and tradition provide a useful framework for faith exploration for our contemporary age where there is a searching after meaning, purpose and truth. This framework allows individuals to explore faith through scriptures, to grapple and think for themselves and allow God's Holy Spirit to enlighten them through this process. While Christian faith, and belief in particular, is not about reasoning through a set of presuppositions, neither is faith blind belief; how we think about faith matters. For me as an undergraduate studying chemistry, I really struggled with the Christian tradition I had grown up in where it seemed I had to absorb all I was told without question. It was not until one day when I was reading my Bible that I discovered that God is actually interested in the way I think, and it is okay to reason things out.[17] This has influenced my thinking about mission within chaplaincy.

For me, mission has to be sensitive and yet have a positive influence on how people live their lives. For people of particular faith communities, it is important for them to understand what it means to be a member of their faith community. For each chaplain of whatever Christian denomination or faith tradition, it is critical that they hold onto the integrity of their own faith while at the same time showing generous hospitality to those who hold different views.

The important thing for me as a Christian who believes that truth is revealed in Jesus Christ is that I have a responsibility to live this out by serving God and the world. A good starting point for me is to remember that the beginning of mission is not our actions, but that God is already at work in the world by the presence of his Holy Spirit. My regular prayer when I start the day is, 'God, where do you want me today?' My work is about joining in with what God is already doing. The apostle Paul exhorts his readers to be faithful in mission more often than to be active.

Over the years, as I have pondered what appropriate engagement in mission might look like within my context I have reflected on different models of mission and have come to the conclusion that an interfaith dialogue model is a good place to start. At its simplest, interfaith dialogue is flexible and takes place between people who hold differing views, in an environment of mutual respect and dignity. Hospitality and embassy are essential in enabling such a dialogue to occur.

This significant concept was introduced in a paper called *Generous Love* presented at the last Lambeth Conference for Bishops from the Anglican Communion (2008). It was the third Lambeth Conference to draw on Bishop Kenneth Cragg's work and writings (the first was 1988 and the second 1998) for guidelines in which interfaith dialogue can take place. Cragg speaks of *hospitality* and *embassy* as two fundamental categories when thinking about mission. Hospitality has to do with welcoming people and meeting their needs. Embassy is concerned with going out and sharing the gospel with them (Cragg 1992).

Kenneth Cragg was a missionary and scholar and is known and well respected for his engagement with Islam. He developed his understanding of mission engagement while working and living in the Middle East. Although he began writing in the 1950s, his many insights are still helpful. As Cragg engaged in Christian mission while working and living as a guest within a foreign culture, specifically Muslim, he needed to be mindful and respectful of his relationship with that country and its Muslim inhabitants. This resonated with me in my chaplaincy context.

Jesus in the Gospels taught his disciples to deliver their embassy within the setting of hospitality. When he sent out his 12 disciples, he told them, 'As you enter a house greet it and if the house is worthy let your peace come upon it.'[18] Likewise when Jesus sent out the 70 disciples, he instructed them on entering a house to say, 'Peace to this house.'[19] The disciples had to receive hospitality and then offer their embassy, which in the first place was the offering of the blessing of peace.

The disciples were the outsiders invited in. In a similar sense the chaplain is the outsider invited in to the workplace. Jesus cautions the disciples to remain with the same people who offered hospitality at the beginning until it is time to leave that place. Paul took these instructions of Jesus to heart and during his missionary journeys he would stay in one place for an extended period of time and he would build relationships and trust. Similarly, as a chaplain to Canary Wharf I have received a welcome and hospitality from the estate owners and the global companies. So as I reflect on the application of hospitality and embassy in my present context, I have made this my *modus operandi*.[20]

Hospitality involves not only the personal inviting of all regardless of faith or background into one's home[21] and as one's friend, but also the openness to understanding their faith or culture – by being hospitable Christ is encountered through welcome and actions.

Likewise, embassy means not only speaking the word of Christ in a 'strange land' but also the determination to be fully 'resident' in those lands and at home where they are... The Christian ambassador aims 'to help the local residents to be more critically aware of their beliefs or values'. In other words, within our conversations we open up to enquiries that enable a Christian viewpoint to be offered.

The Anglican Report, *Generous Love*, reminds us that 'as God pours out his life into the world and remains undiminished at the heart of the Trinity, so our mission is both a being sent and an abiding'. These twin poles of hospitality and embassy are a movement of 'going out' and a presence of 'welcoming in', which are indivisible and mutually complementary, and our mission should practise both (Anglican Communion 2008).

Developing the model for mission and dialogue

As I have practised both hospitality and embassy within my work as a chaplain, I have been very clear that my motivation and integrity in all that I do comes from being a Christian. Even in the early days before I had other faith colleagues, as I worked hard to help the companies to understand that chaplaincy was for all and not just Christians, I was clear that being a Christian was an important part of my role. Since I have had other faith colleagues, one interesting consequence has been that we have all been able to be more open about our own faiths in our conversations.

Hardly ever as chaplains do we begin conversations talking about God, but many conversations eventually turn to God. The Christian example found in the Bible is in the Book of Acts where almost all proclamations of the gospel are in response to questions which prompt an explanation. For example, at Pentecost the crowd asked a number of questions including, 'What does this mean?' to which Peter then responded. Similar to the examples I find in the Book of Acts, I too have also discovered that often in conversations with people I am given permission to explore with them the Christian response to their questions, decisions, struggles and so on.

Conversations with chaplains are ones of exploration together, helping people to understand or ask more questions. It certainly is not about presenting them with a neatly prefabricated packaged faith. The outcomes of these conversations are varied and we are sensitive that people are at different stages of their faith journeys and often our role is to help them take the next step, whatever that might be.

I often use an example from Christianity to illustrate what I mean in explaining that faith is a journey and people are at different stages along the path. The story I recount is that of Jesus travelling on the Emmaus Road with the disciples.[22] There are four stages to their journey:

1. Listening – Jesus listened to the disciples; we too are called to listen first, to hear people's real issues or concerns.

2. Answering questions – Jesus then engaged the disciples in conversation; we too need to be ready to answer people's questions whatever they may be, honestly.

3. Explaining – Jesus then explained to the disciples what had happened, talking them through the scriptures. Within our conversation we can gently help people explore a Christian response to their questions.

4. Choice – what next? When they reached Emmaus, Jesus made out that he was going further; he did not impose himself on the disciples. They chose to invite him in to stay with them. So, too, the task of the chaplain is to give people space to respond, remembering it is the Holy Spirit who transforms a person. Just as the disciples recognized Jesus in the breaking of the bread, so, too, we pray that those who wish to will come to meet and recognize the Lord Jesus and want to become his followers too.

This offers a helpful model and over the years I have had many conversations with people who have been at these stages. In most cases I do not know the outcome, but I thank God for the privilege of being part of someone's faith journey and trust his Holy Spirit for the next step.

Earlier I mentioned that often within the offering of hospitality, we need to be flexible and recognize that the role of guest and host may become interchangeable during a conversation. This is illustrated in the model from Jesus' encounter with the disciples on the Emmaus Road. At the end, Jesus gives the disciples a choice about what happens next. By virtue of the disciples inviting Jesus to have dinner with them they are the host and Jesus the guest, but when Jesus takes the bread and breaks it he becomes the host and the disciples become the guests.

This is essential for understanding the scope of mission in any chaplaincy. There needs to be a willingness for hospitality and embassy to be interchangeable during a conversation or encounter. By this I mean that hospitality needs to be given as well as received. It involves being generous of spirit, being open, transparent and neighbourly. Some of the work of the chaplaincy is with companies and we are on the receiving end of their hospitality. For example, the Financial Services Authority (now the Financial Conduct Authority) offered the chaplaincy a physical meeting space and refreshments free of charge for us to use as and when, but it was important that in using their space we did not abuse their generosity by engaging in activities which would compromise the relationship of the chaplaincy with the company.

As another example of receiving hospitality, Morgan Stanley kindly agreed to help me host an annual ordinands (trainee vicars) training day. Much of the input for the day came from presenters from the bank who facilitated conversations around various financial topics. When I asked them why they would do this with a faith group, they gave the following comments:

> What they [the ordinands] were doing was very important for our society and that, through giving them a sense of what we do in our particular workplace, we

might help them to become still more effective when they become parish priests.

It's interesting for the team here to hear the views of leaders in our communities and useful for us to understand the pre-formed views of the industry by those outside the industry.

Hospitality is about creating or being received into either a physical or virtual space for quality dialogue and respectful listening. As chaplains, embassy means that not only do we speak the word of Christ 'in a strange land' as we minister within a secular context and within someone else's private space, but all our conversations and actions embody the gospel. One of the senior bankers remarked at the end of an ordinands' training day, 'The open discussion…was not only interesting but made us challenge some of our own thinking.'

One of the important features for engaging in mission or interfaith dialogue is a willingness to be challenged about our own beliefs and understanding in our own faith, and often an encounter will help deepen our faith.

What about other faiths?

I have outlined my thinking and reflections on how I have developed engaging in respectful conversations around faith in the workplace from a Christian perspective, while at the same time holding on to the integrity of my faith and knowledge that it is a missionary faith. Islam too is a missionary faith; indeed they are commanded to make every effort to promote Islam and to defend Islam. My Muslim colleague is aware of the nature of the chaplaincy being a guest within the workplace and while he will not compromise his faith or expect members of his faith to do so, he lives out the notion of hospitality, mutual respect and generosity in his conversations and actions as a chaplain. If someone wants to talk to him about what it means to be a Muslim or even wishes to convert, then of course he will assist them, in the same way I would if someone asked about becoming a Christian.

Judaism does not have the issues around mission that Islam and Christianity do, as it is like most other world religions which are not missionary faiths. Although these other religions are not actively looking for converts, it does not mean that people are not attracted to Judaism and other faiths and indeed join them. What it does mean is that my Jewish colleague is very comfortable in offering pastoral care to all people of faith and no faith. We work well as a team and respect each other and this can be seen when we do either stalls at company benefit fairs or 'drop-ins' which raise the awareness of the chaplaincy with the companies. There is a genuine sense of shared hospitality between each of us from our faith traditions and towards those we meet.

While each chaplain understands the sensitivities around mission and the appropriateness of conversations that talk about faith, this is not always shared or understood by the informal faith-based groups within companies. Many years ago a Christian group ran a week of events under the title of 'Christian Awareness' but it was actually a week of evangelistic talks and the company involved was not happy about this. More recently I have been asked by human resource managers to meet with the leaders of their Christian group to assist them in planning events that are acceptable. I will always try and persuade companies to allow me to try and help the faith group plan an appropriate event rather than them saying a blanket no. I think the most helpful way forward is for people of faith to talk about how their faith helps them in their daily lives, how they live as integrated people, whose faith has an impact on their behaviour and relationships within their workplaces, contributing to the core business of the company. That would be preferable to delivering a talk on the beliefs and doctrines of a faith.

Often there is much misunderstanding between people of different faiths and so one of the things we encourage is for the faith groups to learn from each other, and share wisdom from their own faith traditions. One company had a panel discussion working with the different faith groups on the topic 'faith and materialism' and is preparing to have a follow-up panel.

Both ends of the commuter line

I believe that mission in its broadest sense – according to my definition of 'helping Christians to live their daily lives as integrated people, whose faith has an impact on their behaviour and relationships within their workplaces; and when asked using the opportunity to reflect on things from a faith perspective' – must take place 'at both ends of the commuter line'. Another feature of the mission of chaplaincy is working in partnership with local parish clergy or faith communities. A large majority of those who work in Canary Wharf have varying commutes from home, some an hour or two across London and others who commute long distances weekly (within the UK and abroad). From a practical standpoint, when tragedy strikes, such as illness or death or loss of a job, then it is usually the local parish where the person lives which is the faith community best able to support them. Sometimes an enquirer wishes to take part in a basic study course in their faith but would rather do it with their partner at home than in the workplace, so often my involvement as a chaplain is to put people in touch with their local faith community.

I have often prepared individuals for confirmation or couples for marriage in consultation with their local vicar or minister. I believe very strongly that these partnerships are important, especially in the present fragmented international society. For example, a young banker asked to meet with me because he had anxieties about his forthcoming marriage.

At our next meeting he brought his fiancée, then they asked if I would do some marriage preparation with them. They were returning to South Africa for their wedding. Soon after, I received an email with the news that they were being relocated to Perth, Australia, and asking if I could help them find a church. On another occasion, a female banker came to see me for support as she had to make a difficult medical decision. During the following months she started regularly attending our midweek Eucharist, which led to her attending her local church and later to her confirmation. I can think of another woman who asked me if I did exorcisms. I put her in touch with her local parish priest and as it turned out she really needed her house to be blessed, and I understand that she and her family became members of the local church community.

My Muslim colleague tells the story of a young Muslim woman coming to him because her family were struggling with her choice of husband, even though he was a Muslim. My colleague worked with her and her fiancé and their families to help them resolve their differences and was even invited to the wedding, which was in Birmingham. My Jewish colleague has similar stories of how he has supported people or signposted them to their local synagogue, including helping a young man who has converted to Judaism.

Mission for me as a Christian is about enabling people to continue their journey of faith in the Kingdom of God, to grow into mature disciples of Jesus Christ and being willing, when asked, to give people the opportunity to explore faith for themselves. For people of other faiths, I hope that we are able to help them reach a maturity in their own faith that enables them to live as integrated people whose faith informs their whole lives not just the time spent within their faith communities. As people become more mature and comfortable within their own faith we hope that they are hospitable to people from a different faith or no faith and contribute to the workplace in terms of their behaviour and wisdom.

Having touched briefly on the reality that chaplaincy cannot operate in isolation from local communities where people live, given the commutes that people have to Canary Wharf, in the next chapter I will explore why chaplains need their faith communities and why faith communities should value their chaplains.

6

Why Faith Communities Need Chaplains and Why Chaplains Need Faith Communities

Increasing visibility of chaplains

When I first became a university chaplain, I was constantly being asked what was the difference between a vicar and a chaplain. I still get asked this question. The short answer I give is that all Church of England vicars and chaplains are priests but serve God and the church in different contexts. A vicar will be based within a church in the parish and a chaplain usually works outside a church building in the community, for example in schools, universities, hospitals, prisons and businesses. However, the boundary is blurred, as some parish clergy are also involved in chaplaincy work too.

I remember nearly 20 years ago a parishioner in the church where I worshipped on a Sunday saying to me when I announced I was leaving one chaplaincy role for a new one, 'Won't the bishop give you a proper job?' While it seemed quite natural to me to move to another chaplaincy role, I was surprised by the disconnect and lack of understanding often at a parochial level about the role and work of chaplains. While today the church recognizes the importance of chaplaincy, often by its actions and focus it can be perceived to be exclusively parish or church centric. Yet nowadays probably the majority of the UK population is more likely to encounter a chaplain during their day-to-day lives than enter a church.

I meet people whose lives have been touched by military chaplains, university chaplains, school chaplains, hospital and hospice chaplains and yet few of these people attend 'formal' church regularly. Many of the security staff at Canary Wharf are ex-military and call me 'padre' given their experience of military chaplains, and they welcome chaplaincy in the workplace. Workers seek me out because they remember the chaplaincy from their university days. As chaplains we often accompany someone only for a short period of their lives on their faith journeys, but we are there for the times when they need support or encouragement for that period. We very rarely see the seeds of our work come to fruition. A chaplain needs to be able to be comfortable with being part of the journey and hardly ever seeing the end.

In the last couple of years two pieces of research have been commissioned to review the work of chaplaincies within the UK in recognition that the number of chaplains is continuing to increase, both for Christian and other faiths. Both projects have featured the Canary Wharf Multifaith Chaplaincy as a case study.

The report, *A Very Modern Ministry* (Ryan 2015, p.6), says in its foreword, 'Chaplains are everywhere, operating in every conceivable sector and from every conceivable religious base, and in increasingly non-religious ones. The proverbial man in the street seems as − perhaps more − likely to meet a chaplain in his daily life today as he is to meet any other formal religious figure.'

The report, *The Church of England's Involvement in Chaplaincy* (Church of England 2014, p.4), says this about the rationale of chaplaincy, 'Chaplaincy is therefore a distinctive ministry undertaken in the public square by representative and authorized ministers, embedded characteristically in social rather than church structures and focusing on the vocation of the church to serve the mission of God in the world.'

Over the years the role of other faiths has increased, in particular the Muslim community, and Faith Matters has produced an important report about the role of Muslim chaplaincy. The report was commissioned because:

> Faith Matters believes that today, this profession is largely ignored in its importance in a world in which people are affected by growing emotional, technological, spiritual, monetary and physical pressures. This report tries to address this and to promote a discussion around Muslim chaplaincy.
>
> (Faith Matters 2010, p.5)

Muslim chaplaincy has grown in importance, especially within universities and prisons, as it plays a key role in providing support on issues such as bereavement, trauma, radicalization and extremism.

Chaplaincy is located at the intersection of faith with faith communities and other areas of life within society. Chaplaincy is a distinctive ministry: it acts as a pastoral presence within diverse communities, it has the opportunity to make a contribution and have a voice within the public arena, and is able to help their local faith communities understand the culture and issues within secular society. This is possible because while chaplains are representative and authorized ministers, they are rooted in social or secular structures rather than within formal faith structures such as churches, mosques, synagogues or temples and so on.

The issues discussed in this chapter are similar for different faith communities and traditions. While I draw on my experience both as a Church of England priest and Christian chaplain, I have also asked my Muslim and Jewish colleagues to reflect on the themes raised within this chapter about community, and their responses will appear later.

Rabbis, imams and vicars – the same as chaplains or different?

The one thing that my Muslim, Jewish and Catholic colleagues all have in common is that they trained for ministry as faith leaders within their own traditions first before becoming chaplains. Although I am making remarks about clergy or faith leaders, I recognize that there are many lay people who will have received appropriate training and authorization to function as lay chaplains (both in paid or voluntary roles) in their given settings, and who make a considerable contribution to the work of the chaplaincies.

So within my own tradition, as Church of England clergy we all undertake similar training whether we are heading for parish-based or chaplaincy ministry. Our training might be residential within a theological college (as in my case), it might be part time while continuing our normal jobs, or it might be, as in the most recent training opportunities, based within a parish but attending theological college part time. Our training equips us in theology and biblical studies to understand our faith more deeply and how to communicate it; liturgically to be able to lead all forms of worship, weddings and funerals; in church history to understand the traditions of the church; and in ethical thinking and pastoral care. Training is usually to a recognized educational standard, normally degree level. When we finish our initial training and are ordained, we will still need a bishop's licence authorizing our ministry every time we change jobs or move to a different location or type of ministry, whether our context is parish or chaplaincy. However, chaplains do not stop being pastors, teachers, theologians, worship leaders, apostles, prophets, people of prayer, pioneers and managers, and we are still required to offer the rituals for our own faith communities.

Both my Jewish and Muslim colleagues in their respective training as a rabbi and imam have undertaken appropriate initial studies to degree level and have continued studying and training within their own traditions. Chaplains are people who work within professional frameworks and bring their expertise to complement other team members.

So far I have concentrated on the basic training that each chaplain receives within their own tradition. Whenever a chaplain begins a new role they need to understand the context and explore how best to minister within that context. We will often need to do further specialized training within our own chosen chaplaincy field. This is the case within hospital chaplaincy, and specialized national training is available. The Workplace Chaplaincy Mission UK (formerly Industrial Mission Association) offers training for workplace chaplains. Often chaplains will also find their own training to fill a gap in their expertise, as in my case I took a very short introduction to economics to help me understand the financial service industry. We as a team do professional development together; some of the themes have been understanding mental health and wellbeing in the workplace, learning the difference between the roles of psychiatrists and counsellors, business ethics and, more recently, a session to help us understand some of the business implications of Brexit. As chaplains it is important that we continue to keep up to date with the constant changes within our particular contexts and ensure that all we offer as chaplains continues to be relevant.

I believe that chaplaincy has to facilitate ministry and mission at both ends of the commuter line. Often in Anglican terms this means that people are commuting for a different diocese to the one they are working in. Chaplains are not solo ministries; we are on the same team as our colleagues who work mainly from within a worship centre or faith community even if they are different diocese. We should be working together complementing each other's ministry. In practice, this means we are all working together and should welcome and respect each other's ministry and trust each other, at the same time understanding boundaries.

Let me give some examples from my experience to illustrate this:

> One evening I was on a train on the Jubilee line leaving Canary Wharf in the rush hour. The train was absolutely packed; I was fortunate to get a seat. Standing in front of me was a woman who struck up a conversation with me, which began, 'You are the Canary Wharf chaplain?' To which I replied yes. She asked if she could talk to me, and I presumed that meant we would meet and chat over coffee. I was wrong; she continued with the question, 'Do you do exorcisms?' At this point a huge space opened up around us, as suddenly everyone who was standing moved away from us. Feeling this was an inappropriate conversation to have in a tube train I suggested that we meet the next day. On meeting the following day, she explained her concern and as the conversation progressed I was fairly certain that it was not an exorcism that she needed but a house blessing. She said she lived in South London, and it would have been easy to arrange to go to her house one evening. However, I felt it more appropriate that we contacted the local priest, so that he could form a relationship with the family and continue to follow any pastoral needs locally, as needed, with the whole family. Sometime later I saw this woman again and she explained that the local priest had blessed the house and things had settled down. Because the church is about community and relationships, and mission is about building relationships and offering hospitality, for me it was important that this relationship was continued locally with her family and the vicar.
>
> I was involved in supporting two different companies whose main office is in Canary Wharf. They had both contacted me independently after the death of an employee; interestingly both the deaths occurred in small satellite offices of fewer than ten people. For one

company the satellite office was in the Midlands and the other was in Brussels. In both instances I met with the head of human resources and either the chief executive or a senior manager and we discussed how we might support the grieving colleagues both in London and in the satellite offices. Although it would have been possible for me to go to the Midlands office, it was not appropriate because that office needed someone who could offer long-term support. Again, the Brussels office also needed long-term and local support. In both cases I might have been able to argue the case to accompany a member of the senior management team to the local office, but actually in the long term it wasn't me the local office needed. They needed to build a relationship with someone locally. Our role as chaplains is to support the colleagues who are based in Canary Wharf and help them find ways to support their employees in offices located in other parts of the UK or Europe or other places around the world.

As chaplains we can offer marriage preparation. Sometimes a man or woman will come to me a tell me that they are not sure about getting married and during the conversation we explore the issues and often I ask if they have had any marriage preparation. Almost always they say no, particularly if they are having a civil wedding, so often we then offer to do marriage preparation with them. Usually this will involve a number of conversations with the couple covering the following topics:

- How will marriage change their relationship and what is their expectation of each other in the relationship?

- Managing conflict in a relationship.

- The role of money and how financial decisions are made.

- Children – how and where they will bring their children up – including issues, for example, around mixed marriages in terms of nationality or culture, or different faith backgrounds.

- Managing the wedding day if there are family tensions.

Usually the couple then continue with their wedding plans. For some it might mean that the couple are married in their particular faith tradition, or sometimes couples ask for a Christian marriage blessing after their civil ceremony.

Pastoral care should never be about the chaplain. At times it is important to ask the question 'Am I the right person to offer support or could it be done better by someone else or someone more locally?' Or another question to consider is 'Am I the right person or do they need more specialized help?' Crucial to working as a chaplain is the recognition that this is a shared ministry within our particular faith communities and each other's ministry is of value. Occasionally we are asked by local faith leaders to offer support to members of their communities in the workplace, particularly if they have been bereaved.

Faith communities need chaplains to communicate the world to them

> A Chaplain's task…is to translate and interpret the beating and sometimes baffling heart of the world around, be it the university, business, school or church; and to do so from the perspective of Christ himself.
>
> (Stevenson 1977)

I remember at my licensing in Portsmouth Anglican Cathedral as the University Chaplain, the Bishop was very clear in his sermon about the role and task of a chaplain as one of translation of the church to the world and the world to the church. I believe this is true for all chaplains of all faiths – we each have a role to play within our own faith communities.

Contemporary research indicates we continue to become a de-churched (*The Guardian* 2016) nation within an increasingly pluralistic and fragmented society. However, our nation is not only becoming de-churched, other faith communities are losing their adherence too. Chaplains spend the majority of time with people who do not attend a formal place of worship in every age group, and so they are aware of the issues facing people and communities, at work, at home, locally, nationally and internationally.

We live in a global world and all the activities and actions that have developed so far across the world whether for good or ill have consequences which can't be ignored. Forty-three per cent of the world's population have internet access (World Economic Forum 2016), mostly in developed countries. The United Nations has set a goal of connecting all the world's inhabitants to affordable internet by 2020, and whether this goal is achieved or not the world is becoming more interconnected every day. Every day we see images on our TV or computer screens showing world news and events. I am told by people in the global banks that when recent graduates are interviewed for jobs, when given the opportunity to ask questions they are around climate change and sustainability of the planet, and corporate social responsibility. Regularly I get emails or calls from people in their twenties and early thirties who want to be involved in some kind of voluntary work within their local communities. Others have taken a gap year or a few months to be involved in a project in the developing world. These young people are concerned about issues of climate change, justice, health, inequality, peace and human rights. When they ask questions about meaning and purpose it is often not a narrow question about their own existence, but a much broader question about the whole of humanity flourishing and how we contribute to making the world a better place.

On a more local level, not only was the result of the EU referendum in June 2016 unexpected, but also it was a stark reminder that the UK is not a homogenous society and within our own society there are issues around unemployment, poverty, justice, and a north/south divide. In the aftermath I had many conversations about the issues on people's minds concerning uncertainty over employment, whether people's work visas would continue to be honoured and the racism that some had encountered. While these issues might be encountered through interaction with the media and maybe through local congregations, most of the conversations I had were with people who did not belong to a faith community.

Chaplains work in the public arena; they are in effect 'practical apologists' (Pritchard 2007, p.88) for their own faith communities. They can help provide a place where the secular world can meet faith and faith communities. The chaplain as theologian is able to reflect on given issues and challenges that people question about faith outside local faith communities and can give a different perspective. For instance, in my own case I was able to give the church a broader view of the global financial crisis than the one provided by the media. As chaplains, while we are immersed within different cultures and contexts outside the places of formal worship and local faith communities, we must remain critically aware, at the same time assisting those within our chaplaincy context and faith communities to reflect theologically on the issues and challenges faced.

Many congregations within faith communities are not very diverse, with people coming from similar socio-economic backgrounds and having a similar religious outlook on issues facing the church. But individual members of the congregation, particularly within cities and towns, will often be part of a diverse workplace where different cultures, lifestyles and beliefs are experienced, and it might be that co-workers hold views different from the ones they hear at their local faith community or church. Chaplains are at ease in these very diverse and rich environments and can help others understand them and appreciate difference. Global and religious diversity will continue to increase for generations to come, through companies redeploying staff, through immigration and refugee crises caused by world events like war and conflict or poverty. Therefore, the need to understand different cultures and religions is paramount for our society and community cohesion, as is a recognition and appreciation that people of difference bring the wisdom of their own traditions to bear on public debates and decisions.

Chaplains are well placed to communicate these issues to the local faith community or church and contribute to the discussions on how faith can make a difference in today's society. In much the same way that the bank, as I mentioned earlier, had found the feedback helpful from ordinands and how it made them think about themselves, so too are chaplains able to feed back to the church and faith communities 'warts and all' about how they are perceived by people outside their institutions and organizations.

The struggle to find a mature faith that helps people to fully engage with the world

My motivation as a chaplain has never been about numbers. It has always been about supporting people in their faith journey, helping them to become mature in the way they understand and live out their own particular faith, encouraging them to grapple with questions such as: what does it mean to be fully human in the work context, what does it mean to love God, love your neighbour and love yourself in every aspect of our daily lives, how do we cope when we discover our faith does not shield us from moral difficulty, and how do we keep going when the going gets tough? We are also there to support when people's faith is not adult enough to help them cope with the demands of their work life. For example, some senior executives have decisions to make which will have global consequences, but they are not able to draw on their basic faith understanding for help. Many business decisions are not black and white; they are complex and need much wisdom. The internal conversation as to what is the right or best thing to do is hard to handle with a toddler faith. These challenges are experienced by many people of faith, not just Christians, within the business community in Canary Wharf.

This is not a new phenomenon and a number of people have spoken or written about it. In particular within my own Christian tradition, Thomas Bergler says that many American Christians today are not sure what spiritual maturity is or how to get there. He talks about the *juvenilization* of Christianity, where people of all ages are willing to be satisfied by what would be considered appropriate spiritually for adolescents (Bergler 2012, 2014). Many of his observations, I think, are true for UK Christianity. Bishop Richard Harries (2002) has spoken of religion keeping people immature.

Within the first few months of setting up the chaplaincy I was particularly struck by my conversation with the Christian group in HSBC, who said that they needed help to think as mature Christians in grappling with issues faced in the workplace. Not long afterwards a senior executive commented in a conversation that the sermons he listened to on Sundays had no bearing at all on what he did for the rest of the week. Over the weeks and months that followed I heard similar comments, in particular from people in senior or middle management positions. Interestingly, I heard similar criticisms from Muslims about their Friday sermons and indeed, my Muslim colleague has been addressing this issue with Muslim groups for their Friday prayers within Canary Wharf. Others lamented that their church never prayed for people in the workplace; any prayers relating to work were either for the unemployed or those about to lose their jobs. I still remember when I was a curate the young executive who said to me after church, 'Who prays for me? I have to make 100 people redundant tomorrow.'

As a chaplain, I have many conversations with people who tell me that they once were very involved with the church and initially felt welcomed and had a good experience, but who no longer attend. They give me a variety of reasons, such as: the church did not value them or their gifts and talents; they had gone through a crisis of faith related to an illness or a death in the family; they were struggling with issues around sexuality; or they are trying to make sense of a major change of circumstances like losing a job. Others had left the church because it seemed irrelevant to their daily lives or they had outgrown what the church could offer them. As the conversations progressed and as our relationship grew, I often discovered that the person had not lost their faith entirely. Sometimes I realized the person, in fact, had a mature faith. Some have taken part in one of the many Christian basics courses on offer and enjoyed it, but felt they had not been helped to grow beyond it.

I believe that the Christian Church in particular but also other faiths need to address the issue around retention and helping their adherents to have a deeper and more mature understanding of their faith. As chaplains we have discovered in the context of the Canary Wharf estate one of the reasons that fewer people engage in formalized religion is the disconnection between its formal worship activities and the rest of the week. Single or divorced people tell me that they do not feel that they fit into the church community of mainly young families. Others say that once their children had left home they too no longer felt part of the church. In general, it is the 45-plus age group[23] that feels disenfranchised. The observations I have made about Christians leaving the church are also shared with other faiths, in particular my Muslim colleague and I often chat about the difficulties in the Muslim faith, where their members too fall away from their worshiping communities and stop engaging.

I have shared my experience and observations with church leaders, and often we talk about evidence. I was curious to see if there was any research done, as this was not just a phenomenon I was seeing in my context, some of my friends were also expressing similar dissatisfaction. So here is a brief Christian excursion into sharing the evidence I found during my sabbatical in 2014. One example I found was the qualitative and quantitative research carried out by Willow Creek Ministries in the USA (which incidentally has influenced models of church growth within the UK). This research is reported in the following publications: *Reveal* (Hawkins and Parkinson 2007) and *Move* (Hawkins and Parkinson 2011). Interestingly, the survey was carried out when the church was growing numerically. Some of the results were unexpected and a surprise. For instance, it was discovered that there was a large mismatch between an increase in church activities and the spiritual growth of individual members. It was also discovered that there was a significant group of people who were considering leaving the church – some who had done their basics course but not grown in their faith and others whose faith was at the centre of their lives, but who felt let down by the church. Both groups said they were looking for more challenging and theological teaching to help deepen their faith. As a direct result of this research Willow Creek Ministries changed its understanding of church growth, from the numerical 'how many?' to the spiritual 'how are people growing in their faith?' There are other examples, which are well documented (Smith and Pattison 2014; Aisthorpe 2016), but for the purpose of this discussion one example is sufficient.

People belong to a number of communities – the local faith community is an important one

Growing into a mature adult in any faith is a lifelong process, and indeed the Christian word 'disciple' simply means 'learner'. Although we live in a secular culture that emphasizes lifelong learning, often our learning about faith can become stagnated. We learn in a number of ways through individual study, and as part of a community through discussion, shared knowledge and experience. We are relational beings and need to be part of a community. Within the business world it is surprising to discover that the Millennials, who are the most technological savvy generation, really dislike online learning packages and much prefer face-to-face group learning; they need and want physical social interaction.

We all are part of a number of different communities at work and at home. For some it will be a formal place of worship, others sports clubs and other voluntary organizations such as the Scouts. Then there are the more informal communities, the group that goes for a drink or a meal after work, the group of friends who meet up at the weekend to spend time together. Community is about relationships, it is about feeling you belong, and spending time with people means that relationships and friendships grow. There are interesting questions to be asked here: what is it that brings people together and what motivates them to continue meeting?

We often speak of belonging and being part of a faith community (such as a church, mosque or synagogue). It is hard to be a person of faith in isolation; we need each other. Using a Christian example, it wasn't by accident that Jesus had close friends and chose 12 disciples. The early church grew because the believers met socially for meals, but also for learning, and they discussed, prayed and read the scriptures. Within Islam and Judaism, corporate community prayer is very important, indeed required.

I have already given a number of examples of why the local faith communities are important. The local community is not just about helping people explore or grow in faith, it is also about acting it out and caring for one another. If an employee has a member of their family in hospital and needs help, it is the local community which will bring food or offer to babysit.

If a person's role is made redundant it is at home where they will be trying to cope with this change in their circumstances, and often they will quickly lose touch with their working community. Over recent years the Christian Church has placed an emphasis on the workplace given that it is where a large proportion of the population spend their time. However, in my experience, often people might belong to a church community where they work and another where they live, and it is not a case of either/or, but of both having an important role to play and often fulfilling different functions for a person. This is slightly different for other faiths, although Friday prayers for Muslims is an important congregational gathering.

As I have already mentioned, people are looking for meaning and purpose in their lives, which faith can help with, but it needs to be a faith that also expresses itself in active involvement in justice and social issues locally and nationally. People need to understand how to apply the principles of their faith to their everyday lives and how faith makes a difference in the world. There are many churches and some faith communities working together who do this through food banks, credit unions and involvement with local social projects.

Often I am asked the question, 'How do you create community, and in particular a Christian one, in a place like Canary Wharf?' The question usually behind this is, 'Would it help if you had a physical church?' Since chaplaincy is not intended to replace parish churches but to work in partnership with them, I think the question we should be asking in chaplaincy should be, 'For what purpose are we creating community?' When we have a purpose or task, then community more naturally forms. Another related question is, 'Are a number of smaller communities as valid as one big one?' My answer has to be yes. Groups grow around a common interest or concern, as I have illustrated above, so within the workplace there are naturally formed faith communities within the companies, which will include an informal faith network or a group of friends meeting up.

So in terms of the chaplaincy creating opportunities for faith-based communities centred around common interests or concerns, we have limited resources and given the size of the working population (115,000), it is prudent for us to use them wisely. For example, one local church works with many of the companies' informal Christian groups and offers Christian basics courses, so as a Christian chaplain I have no need to duplicate them. Instead, I have put my energies into helping Christians to become confident, mature adult followers of Christ, having an impact on their workplaces by not only their words but also their way of life, through their behaviour, decision making, the way they treat their colleagues and clients, and generally how they contribute to the core business of the company. My other colleagues, too, will use their resources wisely in how they work with their own faith groups within the workplace. It is important for us to listen to the needs of the business community and try and respond rather than second guess what we think they need, as often we can get it wrong, wasting our time and theirs.

One of the areas that became apparent within the workplace was helping people in middle and senior management, as this demographic group has indicated that their local church does not help them to integrate their faith with their work lives. For a number of years now I have been running Faith & Work Forums, which enable people to explore issues they face in the workplace from a faith perspective under the Chatham House Rule of confidentiality (this means that participants are free to use information from a meeting but not to identify the person who said it or the organization they belong to, or to reveal the identity of other participants. It allows individuals to speak freely and therefore facilitates a more honest discussion).

The discussion materials which I helped to develop and we used in the early days for the Forum can be found on the

Faith & Work Forum website.[24] Incidentally, one of the groups no longer uses these materials but a member of the group will bring an issue or topic for the group to discuss.

We do have several Christian worship communities: one that meets for a weekly Mass and another that attends the mid-week lunch break service. Some come weekly, others monthly and others annually, depending on their work commitments. Alongside these physical communities we have a virtual community of people who are linked by receiving a weekly email with a thought for the week based on the reading used at the service, as well as information about special events and other services.

It is people who form community, whether it is a group of two or three or several hundred who have similar reasons for meeting. Some communities will be local to where people live, others closer to the workplace and others still in the time between home life and work life. Wherever people's faith communities are that nourish and nurture them in the faith, those leading them should not fall into the trap of our consumer-led culture where the focus is instant success and experience, because in reality, growing into a mature faith involves a lifetime of faithful service to God and the world.

Chaplains and community: Muslim and Jewish perspectives

Within this chapter I have explored the theme of community from a multifaith viewpoint and commented on some of the issues that different faith communities face. I am a Christian chaplain, therefore many of my comments have been from a Christian perspective. I believe it is important for the reader to hear thoughts and reflections from other faiths and so I have asked both my Muslim and Jewish chaplaincy colleagues to reflect on the theme. Their individual responses are given here.

Rabbi Moshe Freedman – Jewish chaplain

Chaplaincy has been an established and fundamental part of Jewish rabbinic ministry for many years. Historically, it began with army chaplaincy, which continues today, yet that has now been outstripped in relevance by Jewish university chaplaincy, which covers every region of the UK and is prevalent in the USA.

When Jewish undergraduates leave home to go to university, they usually leave behind the links they have to their community and rabbi. Jewish university chaplains ensure that those students don't lose a connection to their Judaism completely. Apart from working to attract Jewish students to events that are of both a religious and social nature, chaplains are responsible for their pastoral needs. This means that chaplains primarily can help Jewish students retain a connection to their religious roots and help to safeguard their future as part of the Jewish community.

Chaplains also play an important role by liaising with Jewish student organizations such as the Union of Jewish Students (UJS) and individual Jewish societies (JSocs). They often play a critical supporting role in guiding and assisting the student JSoc leaders to run events.

Given that religious Jewish students are usually self-organized, motivated to connect with local communities where they study and maintain a connection to their home community, they are generally well catered for. Consequently, while chaplains spend some considerable time arranging informal educational programmes, the majority of the JSocs and chaplains work to engage with non-religious students by focusing on social events and pastoral care, rather than educational programming.

Other roles include mediating with the university over issues of diversity and inclusion relating to lectures and examinations which are arranged on the Sabbath and religious festivals. Chaplains often have to advocate for religious students who are forbidden to attend lectures and examinations on holy days.

The role of Jewish university chaplaincy has had a positive effect on the wider Jewish community as well. Parents feel relieved when their children, who may not have had a close relationship with their home community, get involved with Jewish student life. As a small community, there is always a concern that young Jewish people will stray from the community. Even less religious Jewish parents would prefer their children to marry someone who is also Jewish. Given the small population of Jews (0.5 per cent of the UK population), parents of Jewish students and Jewish university chaplains share a common objective.

In addition to traditional chaplaincy roles, there are a number of Jewish outreach organizations that engage with Jewish students by establishing a rabbinic presence on campuses with large populations of Jewish students. These organizations emphasize an agenda of outreach, which means encouraging Jewish students who are less religious and are at risk of straying from their religion to maintain and strengthen their faith. Their work is similar to chaplaincy and there has been a recognition of the need for organizations to work together for the benefit of the students.

Jewish chaplaincy remains a critical part of the services provided by the Jewish community and aims to bring the synagogue out to Jewish students, while helping to secure the future of the Jewish community. This has influenced the model I am beginning to develop as the Jewish chaplain to the business community within Canary Wharf.

Shaykh Ibrahim Mogra – Muslim chaplain

Muslims employed within the British workforce often find the work environment and the dominant, largely secular and liberal culture within their company quite challenging when it comes to dress, diet, worship and managing conflict between religious law and belief and the requirements of their job or the expectations of their employers. Relating to the opposite gender has also been known to cause challenges for them. A staff Christmas party may seem quite a normal thing to organize within companies but for many Muslims this poses many challenges. A Muslim working at a till in a supermarket would have to handle alcohol and pork, both forbidden in Islam, and this has been an issue for some. There are many other examples of how employment and religious beliefs and practices may collide. The same is true for Muslim students in colleges and universities, Muslim patients in hospitals and Muslims in prisons and the armed forces. These examples illustrate the need for guidance to Muslim workers as well as their employers. I believe the presence of a Muslim chaplain would be of tremendous help.

Muslim chaplains need Muslim communities primarily as recipients of their services. Muslim communities are important as they give credibility, authenticity and authority to the chaplains from their communities.

There is very little religion in the public space and there is even less in business, education and public institutions. Work patterns are always very prohibitive for Muslims wanting to pray regularly five times a day. A Muslim chaplain would be in a very advantageous position to help facilitate and organize all the religious needs that are required and requested by Muslims. They can be there to provide not only pastoral care but also individually tailored spiritual care and guidance.

They can be a good role model and example, especially for the younger generation. They can encourage them to practise their faith and be wholesome individuals, reminding them that they do not have to leave Islam at home or at the door when they come to work, study or play.

Muslim chaplains can demonstrate how the UK provides complete religious freedom to people of a religious and faith background. They can show how religious teachings can help them be better at what they do by displaying honesty, integrity, commitment and dedication, all of which Islam teaches and companies require, or at least expect.

Shared experience with multifaith and multicultural communities

The Church of England as the church by law has sought to build relationships both with other Christian denominations as well as other faith traditions. Turnbull and McFadyen (2012, p.98) remark that, 'The Church of England has a representative and protective role on behalf of all people of faith. But without that presence the danger is that all faith matters would be reduced to the margins of public life.' Anglican churches in cities are often in multifaith and multicultural parishes, with other church denominations and other faith places of worship.

However, from working with other faith colleagues, many chaplains have a wealth of experience and accumulated knowledge that they can share with city or town centre faith communities about how to creatively work with leaders of other faiths and to assist the faith communities in working together and learning from each other.

An example of this, given my expertise gained over the years in emergency planning and critical incidents, I was asked by my bishop to take on the role as coordinator for emergency planning for the churches within the deanery. This role involved working closely with the emergency planning officer (EPO) for the London Borough of Tower Hamlets (LBTH). Together we worked closely, as he realized the network of Church of England parishes covering the borough (and to an extent the Catholic parishes) were in a good position to build relationships with their local faith communities and so extend his network for getting information and support to the right places in the event of an incident happening. The majority of faith communities in LBTH are Muslim, but not exclusively and there are others within the borough including Jewish, Sikh and Buddhist. The Muslim community is also not one homogenous community but several, formed from different nationalities and cultures. A local understanding is therefore useful in helping the EPO to use different approaches with different faith communities.

Important to the work within the borough is the Tower Hamlets Interfaith Forum. The Chair has worked hard over the years within the community to establish the forum because he believes that faith matters to the wellbeing of everyone in the borough. He says, 'The collective power of our numerous faiths is the first step towards fulfilling their potential as a force for positive change and community cohesion.'[25] As a chaplain I am a member of the forum and not only do I bring my experience of working with a multifaith team and the various informal faith networks, but also I learn from the forum. Over the years the faith communities have gathered to support each other, notably when a fire burnt down the local Sikh Gurdwara, and in recent years during the local Tower Hamlets 'No Place for Hate' campaign to combat prejudice, which aimed to stop those who, because of hate or ignorance, would hurt anyone or violate their dignity and to reach out to support those who are targets of hate. The Christians and Muslims in particular have come together in response to a number of attempts by the English Defence League to march through the borough.

To build a multifaith chaplaincy team it has been important to bring into the team people experienced within their own faith and who are comfortable working with people of other faiths. I am fortunate to have a team of colleagues who have considerable expertise within the interfaith arena in their own local and faith communities; they all bring this experience to bear on our work with an internationally diverse multicultural and multifaith working community.

My Muslim colleague Shaykh Ibrahim Mogra has considerable national and international experience in deepening interfaith relations. He was elected as an assistant secretary general of the Muslim Council of Britain in 2008, he is chair of Religions for Peace UK, an advisory board member of the Three Faiths Forum, and a member of the Congress of Imams and Rabbis for Peace and the Christian Muslim Forum. He also contributes regularly to the media, including printed publications, and is regularly involved in national and international gatherings.

My Jewish colleague has written, lectured and broadcast on a variety of subjects, specializing in the conflict between science and faith. He is involved with the Catholic Bishops' Conference as a member of the Catholic–Jewish relations committee and a member of the Board of Deputies committee for Christian–Jewish relations. My Catholic colleague brings his extensive experience of different contexts and varied communities both ecumenically and in interfaith work.

Over time, the team has been asked to participate in interfaith events within the local community; for example, the Canary Wharf Multifaith Chaplaincy was asked to provide support for a bid from the School of Business and Management at Queen Mary College, University of London. It was in the process of submitting a tendered bid to provide a short training course to a group from Bosnia and Herzegovina and thought it was important to include a session on acceptance and inter-ethnic and inter-religious relations within businesses. The group it was looking to work with was made up of about 15 to 20 early to mid-career professionals from a range of sectors, including the media, non-governmental organizations, think tanks, business leaders and parliamentarians from Bosnia and Herzegovina. Since the original bid, the Business School has run the programme on several occasions and we have been involved in delivering the faith session.

And finally

Chaplains working with their own faith communities ensure that the chaplain and their community are the richer for it. The chaplain can bring the world and all the issues that people face within their place of work, or how people are discussing issues on the street back into their local community to help them engage with the world. Local communities can support and encourage the chaplain in their work outside the normal faith structures, as well as providing a platform to think through issues and themes theologically within their communities. The chaplain acts as a translator of their particular faith community to the world and of the world to their particular faith community.

7

Where to from Here?

In writing this book I have argued that far from disappearing from our society, faith is still very much present and an important part of many people's lives as well as active in the public arena. It is my hope that business leaders and faith leaders will read this book and that it also might prove useful for anyone whether they have a faith or not. I have explored the role of faith from within the workplace and in particular my own context, which is a multifaith and multicultural international business community within the financial services sector.

Understanding the role of wealth, money and the economy is complex and yet it is part of our everyday lives. If I have learnt anything working as a faith leader and a chaplain within the financial services sector, it is that the economy is complicated by so many interrelated connections. An example of this would be the sequence of events that occurred when the American bank Lehman Brothers filed for bankruptcy in 2008. It signalled the beginning of a global financial crisis and the implications and fallout that followed were unprecedented. Not only did this lead to the need for tax payers' money to bail out the banks, but also the loss of tax revenue. I remember being told at the time that Lehman Brothers was one of the largest contributors of corporation tax to the Treasury, and its collapse would have left a big hole in the Treasury budget.

Another example would be shareholders. A consequence of the global financial crisis has been the criticism of shareholders. Many of us will have listened to all the arguments and even agreed with them until, however, we have understood that shareholders are not all individuals getting rich, but many are pension funds trying to get a good return on their investments to ensure that pensioners continue to receive a pension. By implication, this means that if we are paying into a pension we are shareholders. Being a shareholder also carries a risk, as the values of the shares can fluctuate up and down depending on the markets.

A major impact on economic and social welfare will be the UK government's implementation of Brexit, as a result of the referendum to leave Europe. While this was a national decision by the people of the UK, I was surprised at the extent to which it was a global issue and other countries were concerned about how their own economies would be affected. It will be interesting to watch as the government continues to work out the implications over the coming years. The exit process is expected to take place by 2019 (although the general opinion is that it could take much longer), and it will be interesting to observe how this plays out on the global stage, considering the UK is at present (2016) the fifth largest economy in the world. The UK is part of global bodies such as the G7 and G20. The membership of the G20 comprises the finance ministers and central bank governors whose role is to ensure that global economic forums and institutions work together. The Managing Director of the International Monetary Fund and the President of the World Bank, plus the Chairs of the International Monetary and Financial Committee and the Development Committee, also participate in G20 meetings on an ex-officio basis.

It is my hope that business leaders will appreciate the positive impact faith can have on the workplace, and that members of the particular faiths and their leaders are encouraged to think more deeply and theologically about their faith and public life, in particular economic life. My plan in this chapter is to follow the principle of 'open questions' and suggest themes and topics to the reader as food for thought on some of the issues and theology relating to economic life. I will give a few pointers and suggestions but will not undertake a comprehensive treatise – that is up to the reader or group to explore.

What does it mean to be part of the human race in today's world?

In Chapter 1, I described the complex global world that many of us live in, and before we consider issues around wealth, money and the economy, a good place to begin is to explore the meaning behind being part of the human race today.

Humans are socially and historically rooted. We belong to particular societies, cultures and communities in a certain time in history. Our genes and place of birth help to define us; we did not choose to be born female or male, or born in Germany or China or Uganda. We did not choose to be born in a developed and developing country, and therefore those of us who are privileged need to appreciate what we have and where we are. As human beings our life depends on ecological systems and interrelated and interconnected structures. We do not live in isolation but in relationship, we form bonds, we learn to trust other humans. Being truly human and living in a community are inseparable. This wisdom is captured in an African proverb: 'I am human only because you are human' (Migliore 2014, p.149). Communities often survive difficult times because they work together and look out for each other. Human beings are free to think and act; they can be rational and irrational and are free to make choices.

In Chapter 4, I referred to the Golden Rule to be found in most world faiths, 'do unto others as you would want them to do to you'. This is a good place to start in reflecting on what it means to be human and our connectedness and responsibilities as part of the human race. It is hoped that each faith community will want to develop this in their own tradition.

Here is an example from a Christian perspective. We believe that humans are created in the image of God, so this is the starting point for our theology of what it means to be human, and we believe that Jesus Christ is the fullest expression of what God intended humanity to be. Therefore, to be truly human means living in a faithful response to the grace of God, it means to live freely and gladly in relationships of mutual respect and love, reflecting the life of God who lives eternally, not in solitary existence but in community. Love is at the heart of the Christian faith and it might be helpful to reflect on the greatest commandments found in the Gospels: 'He [Jesus] answered, "You shall love the Lord your God with all your heart, and with all your soul, and with all your strength, and with all your mind; and your neighbour as yourself."'[26] This is not dissimilar to the Golden Rule.

Being created in the image of God brings with it the hope of God's promise to bring in his Kingdom, the hallmarks of which are faith, hope and love. These are the gifts and practices of a new human relationship with God, a new way of being in solidarity with others, a new expectation of God's reign, grounded and nurtured in the love of God, the faith we have in Christ and the hope God's Holy Spirit brings.

Within the book of Genesis, the narratives about creation and our Psalms we find that God has given human beings the responsibility for working the land or, as we might say today, looking after the world in which we live. Human beings are seen as officials in the administrative arrangement of the Kingdom of God. They are under God's authority and they have been given authority, the nature of which is founded within relationships. God has established dominion over chaos and brought forth creation; humanity is given the capacity and vocation to rule over the animals and bring forth civilization, if we mean by civilization the huge project of stewardship of the world.

Once we have begun to understand our relationship with other human beings and creation this should help us reflect more deeply on the complex issues of economic life, justice and fairness in today's world and our responsibilities and role within it.

Here are some questions to reflect on:

- What does loving God mean? What difference does it make?

- Who is your neighbour? How do I demonstrate love towards them?

- What does it mean to love self?

- What does it mean to be fully human in both contexts – in church on Sunday and in the workplace?

- Christians are called to participate in the world. How do I live responsibly, ethically, humanely and wisely in today's complex world?

- Was does human dignity look like?

We often hear the phrase 'the common good'. I wonder how you as the reader might interpret this phrase every time you hear it. I would suggest that it comprises two facets. The first is providing conditions so that every human being is able to thrive and flourish; these include, for example, peace, security, order, healthcare, education, clean water and necessitate shared public effort by individuals, society and governments. The second is to ensure that the poor, the vulnerable and the marginalized are not forgotten and every effort is made to help them at least attain these elements to an acceptable minimum.

Economy and wealth

When I was on sabbatical in 2014 and working on the two articles that have formed the foundation for this book, I was privileged to meet Professor Daniel Finn, who is both a theologian and an economist. We discussed how Christians make informed decisions about economic issues and activity. He argued that if we are going to understand economics today we need to understand the history of Christian views on economic life. He says, 'Our engagement with ancient Christian texts on economic life must be part of the conversation about the economy today' (Finn 2013, p.4). It is, however, not my intention to enter into a detailed discussion as Daniel has already done so in his book, *Christian Economic Ethics: History and Implications*, which I thoroughly recommend as a good starting point and is a very accessible textbook for individuals or groups to read and discuss.

Capitalism

Since the global financial crisis there has been much debate and discussion around the role of the capitalist market economy. Many would suggest that the market at its worst is unjust, abusive, destructive and prone to crises, and this generation has experience of this. However, when it is at its best, it works well and benefits humanity. China, India and other Asian economies have benefited from wealth creation through the markets, seeing extraordinary gains for hundreds of millions in previously poor societies. Granted there is much more for these societies to do and the media is good at reminding us about the poverty still experienced, but the good news stories need to be told too. Stephen Green says:

> Churchill's famous defence of democracy – 'the worst form of government, except for all those other forms that have been tried from time to time' – applies equally well to the market. It is the worst engine of economic and social development. Except for all those others that have been tried from time to time.
>
> (Green 2009, p.127)

The bigger conversation that should be taking place is how capitalism for the twenty-first century can be reformed with a renewed morality. The Scottish social philosopher and political economist Adam Smith, in his discussion around capitalism, always assumed a deep moral conviction sustaining economic and social activity. Indeed, a renewed morality and accountability have begun to influence the operations of the financial service industry in terms of changing internal culture, improving the values and ethical basis on which business is conducted. As I mentioned in Chapter 4, some of this is through the imposition of the regulatory bodies and some is a recognition by the industry that having a renewed morality is important and makes good business sense. Good morality and business practices are the responsibility of each employee, not just managers enforcing a way of working.

There are questions to reflect on, such as:

- What does it mean to be a good manager?

- What does it mean to be a good employee?

- What are my criteria for the decisions I make and can I justify them?

I have often mentioned as we have gone along in this book that within the business world decisions are not black and white. For a capitalist economy to operate there are hard decisions to make, such as how to balance the relationship between employment and inflation. There is always the battle to keep high unemployment and low inflation, and hard choices have to be made which might mean a higher level of unemployment to keep inflation down, as high inflation affects the whole of society. Yet the ideal is that all who need to work should be able to find employment.

We are all caught up in the economic cycle: we work (or our partner works), we spend money on goods and services, that creates the economy, which then creates jobs and therefore increases the amount of money that can be spent, and so the circle continues. There is another strand to creating wealth, in that not only do we have the freedom to spend our money on goods and services but also we are required pay tax which then finances health, education and social care and so on.

I asked a banker recently why, as a result of Brexit, did the Governor of the Bank of England reduce the interest rate. He replied that it was to keep the country out of recession, which would have a negative impact on our society, for example high unemployment, which then has other knock-on effects. So a lower interest rate is to encourage people to spend money and keep the economy going. This decision, however, is not helpful to savers. On a daily basis, people make hard choices for the common good.

Within our faith communities we might want to explore the role of regulation and laws within our faith. As a Christian it would be appropriate to do this alongside the examples we have from the Gospels of Christ's example of justice, compassion, love and grace. The following questions could be adapted for different faith traditions:

- What do the scriptures say about human beings and their relationship to the law of the land?

- What do the scriptures say about law and grace?

- How does my faith help me to form good reasons and arguments for my decisions and actions?

- What are my/our responsibilities?

- How does what we do impact the wider community?

- Is it possible to ensure the common good of all?

Wealth creation

There is nothing morally wrong with making money – money is important for societies to function and flourish, for families and individuals to live. Wealth is a resource to supply and fulfil human need. Even Jesus and his disciples were supported through his three years of ministry by a group of wealthy women, who made his ministry possible.[27] Paul, during his missionary journeys, stayed in wealthy people's homes (they would have needed to be wealthy to have a spare room). The Prophet Muhammed at the age of 25 married a wealthy widow.

So often over the years I have heard the parable Jesus told in Matthew's Gospel of the rich young ruler to justify why wealth is wrong. But Jesus did not condemn wealth and that was not his reason; the issue for the young man was one of priority, as his wealth had become his God, he had broken the second commandment and wealth had become his idol.[28] The world needs wealth and money to enable people to live and support those who need help. It is all well and good to have a philosophy for looking after the poor, sick and vulnerable but this costs money.

In thinking about wealth there are two fundamental issues to ponder. First, is consideration of the theological principles that might guide how wealth is created. Admittedly, when the Bible or other religious scriptures were written most of the community would have worked the land. Since the industrial revolution, as countries have economically developed, we have lost a sense of direct connection to the land in our cities. Many of us are much further along the chain away from the soil. For example, computer programming draws on minerals mined from the earth's crust, legal systems are attempts to live respectfully on the land with one another, and all kinds of work are exchanged for food and resources reaped from the land. Literally everything we find on the earth, all our produce and all our products, has come directly or indirectly from the earth. In the twenty-first century we have a much more complicated economy, especially those of us who live in the cities and a long way from the land, although it is no less important.

So some reflection around the following might be helpful:

- How does the creation of wealth increase resources for society as a whole, improving the quality of life rather than just creating wealth for its own sake?

- What are our responsibilities as humans in relation to society and the creation/ecology/environment and principles governing economic growth and wealth creation in a world of finite resources?

- What are the factors which influence economic growth, wealth creation and the developing world?

A theological issue that might be useful to explore is how different faiths regard the role of charging interest. Christians might like to explore the theology of John Calvin during the Reformation, which helps to understand our economic system of banking and interest. Followers of Judaism and Islam have different views, and indeed exploring the theology behind Islamic Sharia banking may be helpful.

The second fundamental principle about wealth to consider is that with wealth comes responsibilities, so how do we spend our wealth, not just as individuals but as a faith community, a national or local government, a grant making body and so on? What criteria do we use for the difficult choices? When money is tight, what criteria might we use to make cut-backs and where might we make them?

The decisions on how we spend our money are influenced by our personal ethics and values. For Christians, a strong influence is the theology around the Kingdom of God. This also is a strong central theme in the Hebrew scriptures as well as being at the heart of Jesus' teachings. In Judaism, it would normally be referred to as God's sovereign rule over his people and the world. Within the Gospels, as Jesus teaches on the rule of God's Kingdom, it embraces the whole of human existence. Characteristically, the values of God's Kingdom are those marked by social justice, freedom for the oppressed, fulfilment for the individual and care of God's creation.

Whatever religious background we come from our faith is not just an individual, private matter but should influence every part of our lives and therefore these values should influence every part of our lives, including our own personal wealth, its creation and how we use it.

The role of taxation

Interestingly, on Budget day, why is it we celebrate when tax is reduced, giving us more in our pocket, and yet complain when taxes are raised? It might be interesting to consider a theology of taxation. A starting point in most world religions is the care of the vulnerable and sick within our societies. Before state intervention there was a time when it was the role of the church to provide education, healthcare and social welfare support. Individuals, including Christians, have been at the forefront of funding institutions devoted to human need, such as orphanages, schools and hospitals, to name a few. However, in more recent history, many of these have been taken over by the state (although not all, such as hospices) through other bodies like the National Health Service, and our taxes contribute to the ongoing provision of these services.

Our taxes pay for other things, such as public amenities, roads, libraries, street cleaning, rubbish collection and the upkeep of public gardens. Our taxes also pay for our safety and national security. We have a legal requirement to pay our taxes. But should we do it just because it is a legal requirement? What is our attitude towards taxation?

There is a question here about the person of faith and their responsibility to the country in which we live and all its inhabitants. For the Christian, we are reminded of the conversation when Jesus himself encouraged payment of taxes.[29] Living in a liberal democracy as we are privileged to do, we have a right and a responsibility to participate in the decision-making process through being involved in politics and voting in general and local elections. We can have access to our local Member of Parliament or councillors and we have the freedom to make our views known about various laws and how they affect the wellbeing of society, especially those who are most vulnerable.

Here are some areas to think about:

- What is our attitude towards taxation – what does my faith say about its role? It might be interesting and helpful to review the history of social welfare in the last two hundred years or so.

- Why should I vote?

- What does it mean to participate within the democratic process and how do we influence it in a multicultural society?

Employment and workers' rights

One of the issues I have already mentioned briefly is that of employment or even unemployment. While the ideal would be a state of full employment, without any form of discrimination such as age, disability, gender, ethnicity, the reality is that there will always be a degree of unemployment within a capitalist economy. But this also creates opportunities and encourages entrepreneurs to be creative in new forms of products and services which will go on to provide employment. Our world is continuing to evolve, particularly in terms of technology. I can remember in the 1970s that there was a programme of building leisure centres in the UK because it was thought that with the innovation of computers, people would be working shorter hours and therefore have more leisure time. However, this never happened and instead computers have enabled us to work longer hours, in any location, and have began to blur people's home lives and work lives.

Technology is changing the way we work and live and the nature of employment opportunities. There will always be many jobs that technology can't do for us, but I am sure that continuing advances will bring with them continued change and opportunities and create as yet unknown new industries. For example, before 1998 Google did not exist, but since then website building and apps has developed into a massive global industry.

I have already discussed the role of vocation and work in Chapter 4 and so will not repeat myself here. However, whatever your faith tradition, it might be a useful exercise to explore your own faith more and its understanding of the role of work and employment.

I am sure you can think of many questions to consider related to this, but here are a few suggestions:

- What are trade unions and why are they valued?

- What do we think about paying the living wage?

- What is the difference between exploiting a workforce and valuing a workforce?

- How is a workforce cared for?

These might at face value seem not very complicated issues, and, yes, a big global company will think very differently from a small start-up. Many people in the UK are employed in small and medium-sized businesses, where often finances and budgets are tight. I remember an owner of a small printing company with around half a dozen employees which was struggling to keep going. To keep the company afloat he had looked at all the options and concluded that he had to make one role redundant. It was a hard decision for him to make, and even harder to have the conversation with the person who was just about to lose their job.

No one in today's Western world expects a job for life and many will have a number of different careers. Many within the financial services will have lost their job several times. I was surprised by the number of people who viewed receiving a redundancy package as a positive, and often I would be told that it was the push a person needed to do something different with their lives. Losing a job is not always a negative, but granted for many on lower incomes it will be.

How do we make good business decisions that lead to profit and employment and continued economic growth, while at the same time valuing our employees who make this possible?

Management of personal wealth and money

Our values and ethics should overlap, indeed be of the same standard wherever we are at work or at home. Now we have looked at corporate issues, it is right that we spend some time specifically reflecting on our own pockets, in terms of wealth and money.

Barclays in its values uses the word 'stewardship' as do we in the chaplaincy in the Common Faith Covenant. There was much discussion about what we mean by stewardship, and one definition was 'leaving the world in a better place'. What Christians often mean by stewardship is how we spend our time and money. Both definitions are about how we use our money (and time) for influence – what difference do we make?

I confess that growing up, my theology of stewardship seemed to be limited to giving in the church collection plate! As we reflect on wealth creation we need to have a broader and perhaps more mature view and theology of stewardship thinking about how we use all our money and wealth. Clearly we all have responsibilities, paying the rent or mortgage, paying utility bills, food and other household expenditure, and we all pay tax. But what about those of us who have money left over at the end of each month or are fortunate to be in a job where we receive a bonus?

One of the things I often hear myself saying is that there is a difference between need and want. It is good to understand the difference between necessities and luxuries; it doesn't mean that having luxuries is necessarily wrong but it is about what is important and being outward looking and sharing out of our own abundance.

Often we might not think we are rich, as perhaps we struggle to pay off our credit cards or pay bills, yet we in the developed world are rich, at least in relative terms. Let me expand on this further.

At the height of the global financial crisis I was invited to preach at Leicester Cathedral and the biblical text was the Magnificat or Mary's song.[30] The end of the passage has some very uncomfortable words for the rich and powerful. It heralds a mighty reversal of humanity's understanding of greatness and significance. The proud are scattered, the powerful brought down, the rich sent empty away. Conversely, the hungry are filled with good things and the lowly are lifted high.

As I read and reread the text, I was especially challenged by the phrase, 'and the rich sent empty away'. A week or so before I had led the annual Canary Wharf carol service, in which we customarily give one half of the collection to a local charity and the other to an international charity. This year half went towards setting up five micro-finance projects in Benin, one of the poorest countries in Africa, where people are lucky if they have £1 a day to live on. By comparison, doesn't that mean that all of us in the developed world are the rich ones? God will send us empty away! I began to understand why so few people preach on this part of the Gospel.

When Mary sang her song, it was at a time when the Jewish people had been waiting a seeming eternity for the expected Messiah, God's anointed deliverer.

Mary lived during the reign of Herod the Great, who imposed burdensome taxes that enabled the temple to be rebuilt and also supported his fat-cat lifestyle. He concentrated wealth at the top, took away the people's property and left the masses impoverished. Mary, as a young Jewish woman, knew the scriptures and the promises about the Messiah. The prophet Isaiah, for instance, describes him as the one who would bring justice and righteousness to Israel. So in this context, Mary sings her song of hope in God and liberation for Israel. She sings of the saving intervention of God.

I reiterate my earlier point here – having wealth or money is not wrong; however, within the Christian scriptures we find the following wisdom: it is the 'love of money that is the root of all evil'.[31] So maybe the question to ask of our spare cash, however much or little it is, is how might it benefit someone else who is less fortunate than we are?

Philanthropy

I remember the first time I went to a breakfast meeting in New York when I was on a placement there as an ordinand (trainee vicar). It was a fundraising breakfast and at the end of the meeting everyone without exception got out their cheque book and wrote a cheque for the cause. Philanthropy is in the blood of wealthy Americans; it is second nature. In the UK, before the advent of the welfare state many of our institutions such as hospitals and schools were the beneficiaries of philanthropic endeavours. Indeed, hospices are still charitable foundations.

The encouragement of charitable giving is found in many of the world's religions. It is encouraged in Christianity and Judaism and is one of the pillars of Islam. I wonder how are we prompted to make our decision not only to give a charitable donation but to give to a particular charity.

Often we are prompted to give a charitable donation because we are asked to buy raffle tickets or sponsor someone taking part in an event or we see an appeal perhaps on television.

I wonder how many of us actually sit down and plan what we are going to give to charity for the year. Do we have some criteria to select the kind of things we might give to? It is not about being able to give huge amounts, as every donation counts and is valued, no matter how small.

I am reminded of the story of Jesus in the Gospels:

> He sat down opposite the treasury, and watched the crowd putting money into the treasury. Many rich people put in large sums. A poor widow came and put in two small copper coins, which are worth a penny. Then he called his disciples and said to them, 'Truly I tell you, this poor widow has put in more than all those who are contributing to the treasury. For all of them have contributed out of their abundance; but she out of her poverty has put in everything she had, all she had to live on.'[32]

Within most religious traditions there is a reminder about taking care of the widow, the orphan and the stranger – those who are vulnerable. One of the principles for giving within the Christian tradition is tithing. The Christian tradition of tithing comes from the biblical principle of giving ten per cent of income away to help support the vulnerable and the poor and needy, such as the widow and orphan who had no other financial support. However, in today's world, for example, the Church of England suggests a level of giving at five per cent of disposable income (i.e. after tax and housing costs) as a starting point for charitable giving.

Here are some questions to reflect on for today's local and global world:

- Who is the widow?

- Who is the orphan?

- Who is the stranger?

- How can I help? Remember that giving time as a volunteer can be as valuable as giving money!

- Is tithing still relevant for today? What might be my criteria for how much I give?

Prudent saving and debt

My parents had a mantra which I often heard growing up: 'you can only have something if you can afford to pay for it'. They were totally against what was referred to as the 'never never'. Translated into today's language it would mean not entering into a contract with a company, for example to have a sofa delivered today and defer payment for two years. Their reasoning was that you have no idea what your financial situation might look like in two years' time and what would you do if you could not afford the repayments? I was taught not to live on credit but to be a prudent saver, and save up for what I needed or wanted. The spin-off was that I learnt to value the things I bought and owned.

Many people will buy a property if they can afford the mortgage and this is often referred to as a secured debt because if one defaults on the mortgage the bank can realize its asset by repossessing the property. When we buy properties there are so many things to consider: location, schools, commuting distance to work and value for money. Perhaps there are a few other things too. Do we have to have everything brand new? Does it need to look perfect and fully furnished the day we move in? What can we do without? For example, how many televisions do we really need as a family?

It is prudent to have savings if possible, so that there is money to replace a broken fridge or to pay for a car repair. We all have responsibilities when it comes to our future, and it's prudent to provide for our old age and pay into a pension scheme. I wonder how many of us budget for these things.

Here are some things to consider:

- What are the principles in your faith, which refer to debt as both the debtor and the lender?

- Is there anything in your faith about money management and providing for yourself and partner or family?

- What are our financial responsibilities?

Integration of work lives and faith

In this chapter, I have tried to suggest topics to help equip people to engage with their faith within the workplace. I hope that this will have given some themes to explore with institutional faith communities, such as a church or mosque. When faith leaders encourage and support those who are employed, some of the things to bear in mind with our preparations and how we lead and preach at services might be:

- Do we value the work or professions of our congregations?

- Do we understand their work environment, the stresses and pressures they face?

- How do we pray for people in the workplace?

- How do we support or encourage them?

- How do we help people to grapple with issues they face from a faith perspective?

- How do we equip them to make decisions and take responsibility?

We might also want to think more creatively about how people are encouraged to contribute to the life of the faith community. For example:

- What skills and talents do we have within our faith communities?

- Do people have time to use them?

- Could they mentor others (for example, teachers mentoring and training Sunday school teachers but not replicating their working week by teaching children)?

- How do we help people to be more integrated, making the best use of their gifts and talents both within the local community and at work, neither exploiting nor neglecting them?

When I was a university chaplain, I encouraged our students to ask the priest or vicar at the end of church services questions about the sermon, if maybe they did not understand a point or wanted to explore a theme or topic further. I still encourage those in the workplace to do a similar thing. I wonder when the last time was that you asked your faith leader their advice or help to think through a difficult issue or challenge at work from a faith perspective. Or perhaps you or your faith leader suggested that a group of you could meet together with his or her help to do some theological exploration around the topics that you would like to suggest rather than a pre-planned or generic course.

Christian clergy, rabbis and many other faith leaders will have had extensive theological training and are therefore well equipped from their own knowledge and the wisdom of their scriptures and theological writings to provide insights and to help you explore these issues through sermons or bespoke discussions. All you need to do is ask them. Growing in faith is a lifelong spiritual journey. In Christianity we call followers of Jesus Christ disciples (learners) who are called to do his service in the world. All of us, whether we have a faith or not, are continually on the path of learning throughout our lives as we seek to be the best citizens in this world that we can be.

And finally

The journey over the last years in Canary Wharf setting up and leading the multifaith chaplaincy has been a privilege as well as a huge personal learning curve, and I am grateful for the patience of all those who have journeyed with me. Within this book I have tried to share the story and things I have discovered and learnt along the way. It has been my intention to allay fears and anxieties about the role of faith within the workplace, particularly within global companies, and to encourage real engagement and discussion about how faith can play a positive role within the workplace and contribute towards the core business. I have recognized that not all religious people have a mature or adult faith and need to be encouraged and helped to grow in maturity in their faith, and I have suggested ways for that to happen. I hope I have done this with a large dose of humility, recognising that values, ethics and morality are not the sole preserve of religious people, and at the same time having respect for those who have different viewpoints but equally valid opinions. All this makes for a creative and productive working environment and contributes to the agenda of improving workplace culture and the priorities of the business.

The Golden Rule in Core Religious Texts

Baha'i

And if thine eyes be turned towards justice, choose thou for thy neighbour that which thou choosest for thyself.

Lawh'i 'Ibn'i Dhib, 'Epistle to the Son of the Wolf' 30

Buddhism

Hurt not others in ways you yourself would find hurtful.

Udana-Varga 5:18

Christianity

In everything do to others as you would have them do to you; for this is the law and the prophets.

Matthew 7.12

Confucianism

Do not unto others what you do not want them to do to you.

Analects 15:13

Hinduism

This is the sum of duty: do naught unto others which would cause you pain if done to you.

The Mahabharata 5:1517

Islam

Not one of you is a believer until he loves for his brother what he loves for himself.

Fortieth Hadith of an-Nawawi 13

Jainism

A man should wander about treating all creatures as he himself would be treated.

Sutrakritanga 1:11:33

Judaism

What is hateful to you, do not do to your neighbour: that is the whole of the Torah; all the rest of it is commentary.

Talmud, Shabbat 31a

Native American

Respect for all life is the foundation.

The Great Law of Peace

Sikhism

Don't create enmity with anyone as God is within everyone.

Guru Granth Sahib, page 259

Taoism

Regard your neighbour's gain as your own gain and your neighbour's loss as your own loss.

T'ai Shang Kan Ying P'ien

Zoroastrianism

That nature alone is good which refrains from doing unto another whatsoever is not good for itself.

Dadistan-I-Dinik 94:5

Source: The Tanenbaum Center for
Interreligious Understanding

References

Aisthrope, S. (2016) *The Invisible Church: Learning from the Experience of Churchless Christians.* Edinburgh: Saint Andrew Press.

Anglican Communion (1998) *Embassy Hospitality and Dialogue.* Lambeth Report.

Anglican Communion (2008) *Generous Love.* Network for Interfaith Concerns.

BBC The (2010) *Christian faith plus Chinese productivity.* 27 August. Available at www.bbc.co.uk/news/world-asia-pacific-10942954, accessed on 2 August 2016.

BBC The (2015) *Firm faith: the company bosses who pray.* 6 July. Available at www.bbc.co.uk/news/business-33405579, accessed on 2 August 2016.

Bergler, T. (2012) *The Juvenilization of American Christianity.* Grand Rapids: Eerdmans.

Bergler, T. (2014) *From Here to Maturity: Overcoming the Juvenilization of American Christianity.* Grand Rapids: Eerdmans.

BFO (2012) *Banking and Finance Oath.* Available at www.thebfo.org/home, accessed on 12 August 2016.

Bunting, I. (ed.) (1996) *Celebrating the Anglican Way.* London: Hodder & Stoughton.

Church of England (2006) *Faithful Cities: A Call for Celebration, Vision and Justice.* Report from the Commission on Urban Life & Faith. London: Church House Publishing and Peterborough: Methodist Publishing House.

Church of England (2014) *The Church of England's Involvement in Chaplaincy.* Research report for the Mission and Public Affairs Council.

Cragg, K. (1992) *To Meet and to Greet.* London: Epworth.

Davie, G. (2015) *Religion in Britain: A Persistent Paradox*, 2nd edition. Chichester: Wiley Blackwell.

Faith Matters (2010) *Faith Leadership Through Chaplaincy.* Available at www. faith-matters.org, accessed on 7 December 2010.

Finn, D. (2013) *Christian Economic Ethics: History and Implications.* Minneapolis: Fortress Press.

Ford, D.F. (2014) *The Drama of Living: Becoming Wise in the Spirit.* Norwich: Canterbury Press.

General Synod (2009) *The Implications of the Financial Crisis and the Recession.* 12 February.

Green, S. (2009) *Good Value: Reflections on Money, Morality and an Uncertain World.* London: Allen Lane.

Guardian, The (2012) *Queen says the Church of England is misunderstood.* 15 February. Available at www.theguardian.com/uk/2012/feb/15/ queen-says-church-misunderstood, accessed on 5 August 2016.

Guardian, The (2016) *The Guardian view on disappearing Christianity: suppose it's gone for ever?* 27 May. Available at www.theguardian.com/ commentisfree/2016/may/27/the-guardian-view-on-disappearing-christianity-suppose-its-gone-for-ever, accessed on 3 June 2016.

Harries, R. (2002) *God Outside the Box.* London: SPCK.

Hawkins, G. and Parkinson, C. (2007) *Reveal.* Barrington: Willow Creek Ministries.

Hawkins, G. and Parkinson, C. (2011) *Move.* Grand Rapids: Zondervan.

Independent (2013) *How often do people move house?* 28 November. Available at www.independent.co.uk/property/how-often-do-people-move-house-8969393.html, accessed on 20 June 2016.

Knight, R. (2014) 'Managing people from 5 generations.' *Harvard Business Review,* September.

Lamb, C. (1987) *The Missionary Theology of Kenneth Cragg.* Unpublished, CMS.

Migliore, D.L. (2014) *Faith Seeking Understanding,* 3rd edition. Grand Rapids: Eerdmans.

Mitchell, A. (2015) *Millennials and Political News.* Pew Research Center. Available at www.journalism.org/2015/06/01/millennials-political-news, accessed on 20 June 2016.

New York Times, The (2012) *With 'so help me God' ethics oath, Dutch banks seek redemption.* 12 December. Available at http://dealbook.nytimes. com/2014/12/12/netherlands-asks-bankers-to-swear-to-god/?_ r=1, accessed on 12 August 2016.

Office of National Statistics (2001) *Census Information on Religion.* Available at www.ons.gov.uk, accessed on 23 August 2016.

Office of National Statistics (2011) *Census Information on Religion.* Available at www.ons.gov.uk, accessed on 23 August 2016.

Percy, M. (2013) *Anglicanism Confidence, Commitment and Communion*. Farnham: Ashgate.

Pew Research Center (2015) *Religious Landscape Study*. Available at www.pewforum.org/religious-landscape-study, accessed on 5 July 2016.

Pew Research Center (2016) *News Use Across Social Media Platforms 2016*. Available at www.journalism.org/2016/05/26/news-use-across-social - media-platform-2016, accessed on 20 June 2016.

Pritchard J. (2007) *Life and Work of a Priest*. London: SPCK.

Ryan, B. (2015) *A Very Modern Ministry*. London: Theos.

Sacks, J. (2011) *Biblical Insights into Good Society*. Ebor Lecture.

Sayers, D.L. (1946) *Unpopular Opinions*. London: Victor Gollancz.

Scottish Office of National Statistics (2011) *Census Information on Religion*. Available at www.scotlandscensus.gov.uk/alternative-population, accessed on 23 August 2016.

Siddiqui, M. (2015) *Hospitality and Islam: Welcoming in God's Name*. New Haven: Yale University Press.

Smith, C. and Pattison, J. (2014) *Slow Church – Cultivating Community in the Patient Way of Jesus*. Westmont, IL: InterVarsity Press.

Stevenson, K. (1977) Sermon preached at the licensing of Fiona Stewart-Darling as the new chaplain to the University of Portsmouth, 5 October. Portsmouth Cathedral.

Taylor, C. (2007) *A Secular Age*. Cambridge, MA: Harvard University Press.

Telegraph, The (2015) *Faith integration is bad in Britain; reducing the role of the Church will only make it worse*. 7 December. Available at www.telegraph.co.uk/news/religion/12037784/Faith-integration-is-bad-enough-in-Britain-reducing-the-role-of-the-Church-will-only-make-it-worse.html, accessed on 5 August 2016.

The City UK (2016) *Key Facts about Financial and Related Professional Services*. The City UK.

Turnbull, M. and McFadyen, D. (2012) *The State of the Church and the Church of the State*. London: DLT.

Turner, A. (2009) Mansion House Speech. 22 September.

Volf, M. (2011) *A Public Faith*. Grand Rapids: Brazos Press.

Wallis, J. (2010) *Rediscovering Values: A Moral Compass for the New Economy*. London: Hodder & Stoughton.

Webley, S. (1993) *An Interfaith Declaration: A Code of Ethics on International Business for Christians, Muslims and Jews*. Institute of Business Ethics.

Webley, S. (2014) *Towards Ethical Norms in International Business Transactions*. Institute of Business Ethics.

Woolf Institute The (2015) *Living with Difference, Community, Diversity and the Common Good*. Report of the Commission on Religion and Belief in British Public Life.

World Economic Forum (2014) *Five Ways Faith Can Make a Difference in the World.* Available at www.weforum.org/agenda/2014/07/fiveways-faith-makes-a-difference, accessed on 9 August 2016.

World Economic Forum (2015) *Communities and Civil Society.* Available at www.weforum.org/communities/civil-society, accessed on 2 July 2016.

World Economic Forum (2016) *What Are the 10 Biggest Global Challenges?* January. Available at www.weforum.org/agenda/2016/01/what-are-the-10-biggest-global-challenges, accessed on 17 August 2016.

Further Reading

Atherton, J. (2008) *Transforming Capitalism: An Enquiry into Religion and Global Change.* London: SCM

Bickley, P. (2015) *The Problem of Proselytism.* London: Theos.

Bretherton, L. (2006) *Hospitality as Holiness, Christian Witness and Moral Diversity.* Aldershot: Ashgate.

Cragg, K. (1956) *The Call of the Minerat.* Oxford: Oxford University Press.

Ford, D.F. (2011) *The Future of Christian Theology.* Chichester: Wiley-Blackwell.

Hicks, D.A. (2003) *Religion in the Workplace.* Cambridge: Cambridge University Press.

Jamieson, A. (2002) *A Churchless Faith: Faith Journeys Beyond the Church.* London: SPCK.

Knapp, C.K. (2012) *How the Church Fails Businesspeople.* Grand Rapids: Eerdmans.

Krugman, P. (2008) *The Return of Depression Economics and the Crisis of 2008.* Harmondsworth: Penguin Books.

Legood, G. (ed.) (1999) *Chaplaincy: The Church's Sector Ministries.* London: Cassell.

McGrath, A.E. (1990) *A Life of John Calvin.* Oxford: Blackwell.

Moynagh, M. (2012) *Church for Every Context.* London: SCM.

Newbigin, L. (1989) *The Gospel in a Pluralist Society.* London: SPCK.

Podmore, C. (2005) *Aspects of Anglican Identity.* London: Church House Publishing.

Ramsey, M. (1990) *The Gospel and the Catholic Church.* London: SPCK.

Schwartz, B. (2014) *Islam: A Religion, A Culture, A Society.* Leicester: Christians Aware.

Slater, V. (2015) *Chaplaincy Ministry and the Mission of the Church.* London: SCM.

Sykes, S. (1995) *Unashamed Anglicanism* London: Darton, Longman and Todd.

Threlfall-Holmes, M. and Newitt, M. (2011) *Being a Chaplain*. London: SPCK.

Torry, M. (2010) *Bridgebuilders: Workplace Chaplaincy – A History*. Norwich: Canterbury Press.

Witherington III, B. (2010) *Jesus and Money: A Guide for Times of Financial Crisis*. Grand Rapids: Brazos Press.

Witherington III, B. (2011) *Work: A Kingdom Perspective on Labor*. Grand Rapids: Eerdmans.

Endnotes

1. Canary Wharf as described by the website, I'm Visiting London, www.imvisitinglondon.com

2. EMEA generally covers around 50 countries but the exact number will vary for each company depending on which countries within this designation they operate in.

3. www.food.gov.uk

4. www.theguardian.com/technology/2012/oct/04/facebook-hits-billion-users-a-month

5. www.canarywharfchaplaincy.co.uk/help/faith-work/calendar

6. 'Lunch and Learns' involve a group from the Jewish business community meeting over lunch. While they eat, there is a short talk from a rabbi or member of the group, followed by a discussion.

7. The Khatib is the person who delivers the khutbah (sermon) at Muslim Friday prayers.

8. www.tanenbaum.org

9. www.marketplaceministries.com/ministriesfoundation-whatwedo

10. www.marketplaceministries.co.uk/mission-statement.html

11. www.coexisthouse.org.uk

12. Personal communication with Shaykh Ibrahim Mogra.

13. I was ordained Deacon in 1991; women could not be ordained priest until 1994.

14. www.interfaith.cam.ac.uk/sr

15. We use the word 'stewardship' in the following context: good stewards are people who recognize that their contribution, however small, has the potential to make the world a better place.

16. Personal communication with Shaykh Ibrahim Mogra.

17. Romans 12.1–2.

18. Matthew 10.12–13.

19. Luke 10.5–8.

20 Adapted from Christopher Lamb's expansion of Cragg's twin concepts of hospitality and embassy, *The Missionary Theology of Kenneth Cragg*, unpublished paper of the Islam Panel of the Church Missionary Society, 1987.

21 I use the word 'home' as a generic term that can also mean a space where people meet.

22 Luke 24.13–35.

23 I am aware that it is not only older Christians who find faith irrelevant or stop attending church. There are a number of sources that document this, including David Kinnamen in his book, *You Lost Me – Why Young Christians are Leaving the Church and Rethinking Faith*, published 2011. Within my work it is more often the older age group which seeks out chaplaincy support.

24 www.faithandworkforum.org.uk

25 www.faithintowerhamlets.com

26 Luke 10.27.

27 Luke 8.1–3.

28 Matthew 19.16–22.

29 Matthew 22.17–21.

30 Luke 1.39–55.

31 1 Timothy 6.10; Hebrews 13.5.

32 Mark 12.36–13.2.

Index